THE PERSONAL AND THE POLITICAL

Three Fables by Montesquieu

French-English Parallel Texts

TRANSLATION AND COMMENTARY BY
W. B. ALLEN

University Press of America,® Inc.
Lanham · Boulder · New York · Toronto · Plymouth, UK

Copyright © 2008 by
University Press of America,® Inc.
4501 Forbes Boulevard
Suite 200
Lanham, Maryland 20706
UPA Acquisitions Department (301) 459-3366

Estover Road
Plymouth PL6 7PY
United Kingdom

Library of Congress Control Number: 2008925445
ISBN-13: 978-0-7618-4078-7 (paperback : alk. paper)
ISBN-10: 0-7618-4078-8 (paperback : alk. paper)

Cover illustration by Sandra Woizeski-Wallin,
Montesquieu's Lysimachus,
Copyright the Oldtown Press, Los Angeles, CA.

⊖™ The paper used in this publication meets the minimum
requirements of American National Standard for Information
Sciences—Permanence of Paper for Printed Library Materials,
ANSI Z39.48—1984

Contents

Chapter 1
Montesquieu's *Temple de Gnide*
The Marriage of Law and Reason
Translation and Commentary

Chapter 2
Montesquieu's *Lysimachus*
Translation and Commentary

Chapter 3
Montesquieu's *Sulla and Eucrates*
Translation and Commentary

iv

General Preface

An Introduction to Political Philosophy

Charles-Louis de Secondat, Baron de La Brede et de Montesquieu, was born January 18, 1689 and died February 10, 1755. One of the most celebrated thinkers of the French enlightenment, he is most known for having developed the constitutional theory of the separation of powers in his masterwork, *The Spirit of the Laws* (1748). His early literary career, however, focused upon philosophical fiction more than historical or analytical narrative. In 1723 he published the justly famed *Persian Letters*. That novel length work was followed by the short fables, *Dialogue de Sylla et d'Eucrate* and *Le Temple de Cnide* (1724). In 1731 he published *Lysimaque*. These works appeared, therefore, prior to his historical and philosophical masterworks, *Considérations sur les causes de la grandeur des Romains et de leur décadence* (1734) and *De l'esprit des lois*. Upon his death in 1755, Montesquieu was engaged in editing and re-issuing *Le Temple de Cnide*. He accorded no less significance to his fictional works than to his philosophical treatises.

Montesquieu was not alone in turning to fable in the 18th century, but he was surely its most accomplished fabulist. The ready recourse to moral fable in the eighteenth century contrasts sharply with any approach contemporary philosophers would likely adopt. Further, the claim that such fables might be a vehicle for the development of philosophical principles is in our time contrary to our intuitions. It is no accident, doubtless, that apart from Rousseau's *Émile* the fictions and other romantic creations of serious writers from the eighteenth century and later receive short shrift from biographers, philosophers, and historians.

This interpretation offers non-hackneyed principles of philosophical and political analysis that identify eighteenth century thought on grounds which differ radically from those that prevail in our time and thus stands in a different relation to ancient thought than we would otherwise imagine.

The driving question takes Socrates and Athens as they appear, rather than in the form of Humean revisionism (in his fable, "A Dialogue"), and asks whether the marriage of reason and law is the correct foundation of human ethics.

Seventeenth century fabulist La Fontaine, in other words, did not go so far as Rousseau thought he had to go, but nevertheless left it as questionable whether there remained any guidance for human beings as to ends. Montesquieu by contrast points to the marriage of law and reason as a reasonable enterprise and does not forsake the possibility of providing guidance as to ends.

Though writing in the era of the "social contract," Montesquieu avoids the peril of founding every human society on nothing more substantial than the whims and caprices of humans. Every contract must be referred to its makers for its authoritative meaning. Each maker is always authoritative as to what he intended. The variety of human opinions about the good suggests differing opinions about the aim of a contract—a diversity which cannot be overcome by *post facto* philosophic speculations. The turn to fable is expressly devoted to defending an *a priori* source of authority.

Because Montesquieu's version of modern political philosophy is still closer to the ancient tradition than it is close to contemporary science, it mediates an introduction to philosophy that aims to bridge ancient and modern thought. At its origins, modern philosophy still confronted the fundamental question: whether the sphere of morality is closed or open to the sphere of philosophy. A philosophical morality, so far as there is such, is the ground upon which the philosopher experiences the necessity of concern with the sphere of morality not as a seeker of truth but as a good man.

This runs counter to the more recent tendency in which philosophy becomes the sole standard of human morality: so construed the philosophers are no longer subject to the charge of impiety for which Socrates was executed. For the provenance of piety has become the Nietzschean will of that exalted personage, the philosopher. This move eliminates a perennial danger to philosophy by making philosophy the judge in a dispute to which philosophy is also a party. But that is done at the cost of standards to guide personal conduct as well as political construction.

This work responds to attempts (Rosso) that collapse Montesquieu's analysis into a general discussion of virtue or political morality, understood merely as feeling, by raising anew the issues of true and false happiness and true and false pleasures. Montesquieu's leading makes political philosophy relevant again. His moral fables, and especially the *Lysimaque*, demonstrate the continuing relevance of the issue of philosophical morality. And although the other fables take the point of view of the city, they nevertheless participate in the same discussion. This work accordingly offers Montesquieu's reconciliation of the tension between philosophical morality and political morality.

Finally, the question as to what is the philosophical morality emerges as none other than, what is the golden mean for philosophy. Montesquieu's *Lysimaque* portrays one possibility, while *Gnidus* and *Sylla* round out the consideration. Interestingly, the expressly political fables (*Lysimaque* and *Sylla*) are narrated by a philosopher, while the expressly erotic *Gnidus* is narrated by a gentleman. Taken together, we observe the philosophers moderating their political ambitions and the gentleman enlarging his erotic ambitions, the resulting harmony producing moderation in personal and political conduct.

Acknowledgments

Cover Illusration by Sandra Woizeski-Wallin, 1984. I published it originally as the frontispiece to a fine press edition of Montesquieu's *Lysimachus* at the Oldtown Press in Claremont, California. I republish it now in order that it will have the broader attention it deserves.

I owe thanks to the Earhart Foundation in Ann Arbor, Michigan for support of sabbatical leave at the James Madison Program in American Ideals and Institutions at Princeton University. The time they afforded me enabled me to complete the preparation of this work.

To Carol M. Allen, my partner in work and in life, I owe great gratitude for assistance in preparation of the mansucript.

Chapter 1

Montesquieu's *Temple de Gnide*

The Marriage of Law and Reason
Translation and Commentary

Preface

It is our custom to treat the philosophy of the eighteenth century as the true and lineal ancestor of philosophy in our own time. We are perhaps mistaken, however, in imagining the terms and practices of contemporary philosophy to have been set in the principles of eighteenth, as opposed let us say to nineteenth, century philosophy. If we have been mistaken in identifying the sources of our practices, we at least have not been scandalously mistaken. It were natural enough for a modern thinker to conceive that his principles were derived from ancient thinkers and principles. In spite of eighteenth century thought's obsession with the war between the ancients and the moderns, I suggest reconsidering its foundations, in which reconsideration I quite consciously if obtusely treat the distinction between ancients and moderns as an open question.

While this reconsideration is fit for a general project, I am interested in it via the medium of a quite specific work, within a very narrow genre. This is a clue to guide us. For surely the ready recourse to moral fable in the eighteenth century contrasts sharply with any approach any contemporary philosopher is likely to adopt. Further, the claim that such fables might be a vehicle for the development of philosophical principles is in our time contrary to our intuitions. It is no accident, doubtless, that apart from Rousseau's *Émile* the fictions and other romantic creations of serious writers from the eighteenth century and after receive short shrift from biographers, philosophers, and historians. The *Temple de Gnide* by Montesquieu is no exception. Like many of his other fables, this one generally attracts patronizing praise of its workmanship and neglect of its content.

I believe that a strong case can be made to interpret the *Temple de Gnide* philosophically—as with all Montesquieu's fables. Further, I believe that such an interpretation will establish non-hackneyed principles of philosophical and political analysis that identify eighteenth century thought on grounds which differ radically from those which prevail in our time and thus stand in a different relation to ancient thought than we may imagine. That is why I offer an English translation of the *Temple* de *Gnide* and a brief commentary on it. First, however, I choose to establish the context within which this analysis takes place by reconstituting the language and the problem as they were viewed in the eighteenth century by David Hume.

Introduction

The principal version of the modern predicament that characterized eighteenth century reflection was the fact that recourse to general reason and enlightenment had undermined the traditional association of ideas of the human good with particular regimes. The regime or constitution had become merely instrumental, itself a product of rational purpose but not rational in itself. Thus, morals and social principles came to be seen to depend on "sentiments," as opposed to rational principles.[1] While this eventuality created for some the dilemma that morals ceased to be assimilable to reason insofar as the objects of rational inquiry were still regarded as beyond convention, for Hume it led only to a natural emphasis on utility:

> But to all appearance the sentiments of Stockholm, Geneva, Rome ancient and modern, Athens and Memphis, have the same characters; and no sensible man can implicitly assent to any of them, but from the general principle, that as the truth in these subjects is beyond human capacity, and that as for one's own ease he must adopt some tenets, there is most satisfaction and convenience in holding [that we first were taught].[2]

Where men once held it to be the case that their moral obligations required to be comprehended as necessary, then, Hume maintained that they were adequately accounted for on grounds of utility. In that he eliminated the need for rational justification of moral principles [the term rational justification as used here applies to ends, not to the means selected to secure ends].

Whether it were so or not, eighteenth century thinkers generally considered that the ancients thought differently about these matters. Hume was no exception. In particular, although he was not much of a poet (which Montesquieu certainly was), Hume went so far as to write a fable, "A Dialogue," in which he sought to portray this difference between ancients and moderns and its consequences. We might add that he seemed especially proud of this effort. The point to note here is that the difference which is emphasized is not a difference in perspective on science, *per se*, but rather a difference in perspective on the status of morality— or whether morality could be a proper object [as end] of philosophical inquiry at all (for which sake it must be general or universal as opposed to particular). Hume's fable maintains that the relativity of morals expresses a fundamental opposition between morality (or law) and reason and thus argues against Montesquieu.

Hume's "A dialogue" is an apt vehicle to introduce *Temple de Gnide*. Montesquieu published his fable shortly after his *Les Lettres Persanes* had appeared to welcome reviews. A few of the themes of *Les* Lettres *Persanes* were the focus in *Temple de Gnide*, albeit in a different setting. Nevertheless, *Les Lettres Persanes* was regarded as a serious if charmingly diverting work, while *Temple de Gnide* was regarded as merely a charming diversion.

Temple de Gnide was never regarded seriously, until the publication of "A Dialogue" in 1751 and Rousseau's stinging criticism in *Les Rêveries du Promeneur Solitaire* in 1782. The *Temple de* Gnide goes unmentioned in Hume's fable. I would argue, however, that it and *Les Lettres Persanes* are the probable sources of inspiration for "A Dialogue." The reason for this is as follows: several odd resemblances and parallels among these works, in light of already established evidence of Hume's close reading of Montesquieu (*Les Lettres Persanes* especially) and his frequent, extensive responses to Montesquieu, offer the kind of factual certainty which Hume, above all others, would yield to as probable evidence of a correspondence.[3]

Like *Temple de Gnide*, Hume's fable is narrated by an unnamed character who is also the principal character of the tale. Unlike *Temple de Gnide*, most of the character and place names in Hume's fable are patent inventions, with the exception only of two which play roles of some importance. Most important is the narrator's interlocutor, Palamedes, whose name invokes the mythology of the Trojan War in the same manner that most of the important names in *Temple de Gnide* do. Next is the character Usbek, the single name in a series of artificial names which itself is not artificial and which is the name of the principal character in *Les Lettres Persanes*. Usbek's chief problem in that work (the woman question) is also the chief question of *Temple de Gnide* and also a major theme of "A Dialogue," indeed the main question of the narrator's presentation. Further, Usbek in *Les Lettres Persanes* is the source of the argument in defense of fable as an alternative and perhaps superior mode to convey philosophic truth (also a question in "A Dialogue").

The key to understand "A Dialogue" seems to be the character of Palamedes, called "a rambler in his principles." The fable begins with a parody of Athenian morals and manners related by Palamedes and in which the typical Athenian, the "Athenian man of merit," is Socrates. In relating his tale, however, Palamedes abstracts completely from the cause of death of Socrates and presents the caricature of Socrates's morality as a general portrait of Athenian morality. While the Socrates character, Alcheic, was compounded of events in the lives of Themistocles, Brutus, and Socrates, Palamedes applied all the judgments of this character to the "Athenian man of merit."

> I think I have fairly made it appear, that an Athenian man of merit might be such as would pass with us for incestuous, a parricide, an assassin, an ungrateful, perjured traitor, and something else too abominable to be named; not to mention his rusticity and ill-manners.

Next, he argued, Alcheic took his own life, having fallen "into a state of bad health," "universally regretted and applauded in that country." Hume's narrator considered Socrates's end desperate but suitable, although Alcheic died "with the most absurd blasphemies in his mouth"—he boasted that "a wise man is scarcely inferior to the great god." So much was this approved and applauded at Athens, that

> he shall have statues, if not altars, erected to his memory; poems and orations shall be composed in his praise; great sects shall be proud of calling themselves by his name; and the most distant posterity shall blindly continue their admiration; though were such a one to arise

among themselves, they would justly regard him with horror and execration.

The indictment concluded thus, and it was an indictment in spite of Palamedes's apparent purpose to portray the relativity of morals and manners—their detachment from reason. Perhaps the reason this turned into an indictment lies in the fact that, in forming the portrait of Socrates's character, Palamedes made no use of the single veridical event from Socrates's life included in the tale. That was the story from Xenophon's *Memorabilia,* in which Socrates influenced his boys to moderation by establishing the principle of sharing their meals in common when they dined together. In that story shame was the principle which operated to inspire moderation. Palamedes made it a point to say that he copied the story literally from Xenophon.[4] Nevertheless, he called Socrates's device an artifice, as if to suggest that the generosity, the eye for the common good, which he inspired, had no deeper foundation than transient artifice. It was regarded as "extraordinary" for the very reason that it stood out in stark contrast to the ordinary manners of Athenians and, as he portrayed it, the selfish end of Socrates's life. Thus, it was not a character trait but a momentary self-indulgence.

Now we can see how Palamedes himself serves to unravel the secret of this fable. In his own person, or at least his own name, this character whom Socrates so regularly invoked as the symbol of Socrates's own character and circumstances, denies Socrates's claims. He treats Socrates as the very opposite of himself and thereby tacitly rejects the union of knowledge and virtue. Palamedes had signified for the historical Socrates the unacceptable opposition of law and reason. In Xenophon's *Apology* Socrates deflected the ignominy of his being "executed unjustly" to his executioners, just as he found "far more noble themes for song" in Palamedes's circumstances than in those of Odysseus who conspired to execute Palamedes unjustly. Socarates said that he took "comfort" in the example of Palamedes.[5] Again, in the *Memorabilia,* Socrates made Palamedes the prototype of the refutation of Euthydemus's argument that the good is the beneficial (useful) and the evil harmful (inexpedient), "for all the poets sing of him, how that he was envied for his wisdom and done to death by Odysseus."[6] Palamedes was reputed to be the discoverer of number and the inventor of the Alphabet, lighthouses, weights and measures, dice, backgammon, and the discus, as well as the discoverer of Odysseus's ruse for avoiding service at Troy. Socrates accordingly took his bearings as much from Palamedes's superior reason as the injustice which he suffered.[7] Nor was he alone in his appreciation of that unjust fate.[8] Thus he magnified his own fate and end:

> I am willing to die many times if these things [about hades] are true, since especially for myself spending time there would be wondrous: whenever I happened to meet Palamedes and Telemonian Ajax, or anyone else of the ancients who died because of an unjust judgment, I would compare my own experiences with theirs.[9]

How shocked, then would Socrates-Alcheic be, to meet with Palamedes-Hume and discover that the standards of comparison had changed—to learn indeed that his having lived seventy years unmolested and died only at a time when life becomes unsupportable[10] had become evidence for the fact not only that he was not treated unjustly but had in fact set the standard for a despicable and unworthy Athenian morality? Might Hume have considered Socrates's end a form of unworthy crying, his insistence that knowledge is virtue an unjustified attempt to defend the life he led beyond the utility which he derived from it?

It would be premature to conclude so, for we have reviewed only the half of "A Dialogue." And while it is true that Palamedes concludes the second half of the fable with a statement which echoes this provisional conclusion and relates strongly to remarks Hume makes elsewhere, the fable takes a turn which qualifies the force of this reflection. Palamedes's point is this:

> religion had in ancient times, very little influence on common life. . . In those ages it was the business of philosophy alone to regulate men's ordinary behavior and deportment; and accordingly, we may observe, that this being the sole principle, by which a man could elevate himself above his fellows, it acquired a mighty ascendant over many, and produced great singularities of maxims and conduct.

On this reading the ancient gods had little or no regard for the "virtues or vices which only affected the peace and happiness of human society." In that situation the identification of wisdom and virtue conduced to satisfying the philosopher's utility—he had free scope to seek his elevation. The fact that Palamedes offers this portrait of natural manners *after* a lengthy refutation from the unnamed narrator inclines us to see in Palamedes the mind of Hume, in whom we find an echo of the portrait of "artificial manners" with which Palamedes contrasted the ancient ways. In the essay, "Of some Verbal Disputes," Hume explained why modern philosophers reason differently than their ancient counterparts in matters of morals.

> In later times, philosophies of all kinds, especially ethics, have been more closely united with theology than ever they were observed to be among the Heathens; and as this latter science admits of no terms of composition, but bends every branch of knowledge to its own purpose, without much regard to the phenomena of nature, or to the unbiassed sentiments of the mind, hence reasoning, and even language, have been warped from their natural course, and distinctions have been endeavored to be established, where the difference of the object was, in a manner imperceptible.[11]

In this light, the purpose of "A Dialogue" seems to be to offer in mimetic form a test of the proposition whether the marriage of reason and law or morality in Christianity can be comprehended in an adequate general account of the "behavior and deportment" of humankind.

Since this question, apart from direct consideration of the element of Christianity, is at the heart of *Temple de Gnide,* it is also here that we discern the intersection between the two fables. The question might be restated, taking Socrates and Athens as they appear rather than in the form of Humean revisionism, to inquire whether the marriage of reason and law is the correct foundation of human ethics. That is at least how Hume's unnamed narrator conceives it, despite agreeing with Palamedes in the end, that

> When men depart from the maxims of common reason, and affect these *artificial* lives, as you call them, no one can answer for what will please or displease them. They are in a different element from the rest of humankind; and the natural principles of their minds play not with the same regularity, as if left to themselves, free from the illusions of religious superstition or philosophical enthusiasm.

The "philosophical enthusiasm" which the narrator appends was called "extravagant philosophy" by Palamedes, exampled by Diogenes and Pascal, the latter of whom Palamedes considered as the perfection of Christian example and the former of whom Palamedes used as the perfection of the example of Socrates. From the contrast between Diogenes and Pascal, Palamedes concluded that there seemed no "universal standard of morals." The narrator, on the other hand, considers these both examples of "artificial lives" beyond the reach of common human experience and therefore yielding no general rule.

The narrator initially sought to defend Athenians (he did not mention Socrates) and in doing so educed "four sources of moral sentiments" which subsist everywhere, subject only to accidental variations. These four were the propensities to "useful" and "agreeable" qualities respecting oneself and society. As such they were opposed to Palamedes's fourfold "foundation of all moral determinations:" fashion, vogue, custom, and law. Now, inasmuch as fashion, vogue, and custom are in reality only one thing, common prejudice, Palamedes offers at most two foundations of morality. And insofar as law has no foundation other than common prejudice—his original argument—he offers only one foundation. Prior to deducing his "four sources of moral sentiments" the narrator responded to Palamedes's foundation in common prejudice by suggesting that the single foundation was in fact the universal propensity to praise and blame of human qualities as conducing or not to what is useful or agreeable, for "where would be the sense of extolling a *good* character or action, which at the same time, is allowed to be *good for nothing*." Thus, he insisted on a general, objective foundation for "all the differences, therefore, in morals." The difference seems to be that mere prejudice is insufficient to guide men insofar as they act on the basis of the useful or agreeable. Hence, prejudice gains its power from its ability to *seem* to answer the need to identify the useful or agreeable. Palamedes and the narrator do not seem very far apart.

There is a difference, however. The narrator drew out this difference by concentrating above all on the relations between the sexes and describing moral sentiments as naturally founded in the necessity to follow principles of utility and agreeableness determined by the circumstances. In that light, the variations among men in these matters express an underlying uniformity.

The narrator portrayed a modern people whose manners could be as easily parodied to their disadvantage as those of the Athenians had been. In doing so he drew from Palamedes the disclaimer that he had not designed to exalt "the moderns at the expence of the ancients." The modern people were the French, and their extreme deference to women was the central feature of the narrator's story (and perhaps the heart of Hume's criticism of Montesquieu). Palamedes did not retract his insistence that the Athenian man of merit would be to them a horror, despite the French affectation that no people other than they were ever so like the Athenians.[12] He was, however, willing to concede that the French man of merit might "be an object of the highest contempt and ridicule" at Athens.

Rousseau conceived that the teaching of *Temple de Gnide* was just such a "superiority of the females" as was also described in *Les Lettres Persanes* and which constitutes the central teaching of the French man of merit. The French man of merit was Montesquieu. He sought principles of ethics beyond mere convention, even while conceding the modern principle of utility.[13] Our narrator turned to the discussion of praise and blame to indicate how far Montesquieu might succeed: "the principles upon which men reason in morals are always the same, though the conclusions which they draw are often very different." Everywhere the spirit of law-abidingness is "a capital virtue." Our notions of beauty of person persist in ancient and modern eras, expressed in the Apollo and the Venus, while it is the character of a Scipio and the honor of Cornelia which universally fulfill expectations of heroes and matrons. That is, the *Temple de Gnide's* celebration of the body is just, while its standards of heroism and feminine virtue may miss the point.

The absence of war in Montesquieu's fable may testify to the insufficiency of his celebration of the soul. For it is the "difference between war and peace" which diversifies the most "our ideas of moral virtue and personal merit." In this sense, the closest we approach toward universality is in recognizing "the merit of riper years": "integrity, humanity, ability, knowledge, and the other more solid and useful qualities of the human mind." But *Temple de Gnide* celebrates the "manner, the ornaments, and the graces" of the young, which "are more arbitrary and casual." Given our narrator's concurrence with Palamedes that modern religion has displaced philosophy, with the result that the latter like ancient religion exists but does not care about "those virtues or vices which only affected the peace and happiness of human society," there must seem little or no occasion for reason to guide the morals of the young.

The conclusion of Hume's fable, or something like it, may account for Rousseau's attack on the lasciviousness of *Temple de Gnide*. Even if the fable had a nobler purpose, Rousseau held, it appealed to those passions which, when encouraged, could lead only to harm and which were not susceptible to the restraints of reason. It is not that Rousseau despaired of universal principle. He argued that

La verité générale et abstraite est le plus precieux de tous les biens.
Sans elle l'homme est aveugle; elle est l'oeil de la raison.[14]

One concludes, therefore, that he understood universal and abstract truth
to be inapplicable to this subject, to which strong convictions alone apply. One may deduce as much from the form of his description of the
precise evil of the fable, which, he held, offered under the false mantel
of antiquity a modern poison, at least for the unwary.

> . . . il faut détacher du public instruit des multitudes de lecteurs simples
> et crédules à qui l'histoire du manuscrit, narrée par un auteur grave
> avec un air de bonne foi, en a réellement imposé et qui ont bu sans
> crainte, dans une coupe de forme antique, le poison dont ils se seraient
> au moins défiés s'il leur eut été présenté dans une vase moderne.[15]

Rousseau, of course, argued consistently against the use of fables for
youths. La Fontaine he saw as dangerous and regarded his fables as
useful only for adults. Thus, his criticism of Montesquieu is akin to that
against La Fontaine, with the addition that he sees Montesquieu as offering a frankly modern teaching and, presumably, a teaching consistent
with Palamedes-Hume.

We disagree with Rousseau and believe that the problem can be illus-
trated by a closer look at his understanding of La Fontaine before we
determine on the modernism of Montesquieu. Whatever the degree of
modernism in the fables of Fontaine, at least Fontaine defended himself
against Rousseau in advance. He insisted, of course, that his "apparent
puerilities" were in fact "some important truths."[16] Nevertheless, he
held these truths to be important for children as well as adults—perhaps
more so. He argued, for example, that it would mean little to tell a child
that Crassus in his attack on the Parthians paid too little heed to how he
would exit the country after entering it, and this caused him and his army
to perish in spite of attempting to withdraw. To the same child, he wrote,
say that the fox and the goat went into the bottom of a well to get a drink;
that the fox climbed out upon the shoulders and horns of his comrade;
and the goat was stuck there on account of lacking such foresight. The
child then would grasp the principle of the error of Crassus and not, as
Rousseau maintained, learn how to exploit friendships.

The apparent impasse between Rousseau and La Fontaine may be
resolvable only by recourse to their intentions. Fontaine traced the inspiration of his art to Socrates in Plato's *Phaedo*. When he paraphrased the

discussion of Socrates's dream, which led to Socrates setting Aesop to meter, he added a note: "car, comme la musique ne rend pas l'homme meilleur, à quoi bon s'y attacher?" [for, music not making man the better, what good is there for him to apply himself to it?] Socrates, of course, held that he was unsure whether the gods meant for him to make philosophy or to make poetry, when they commanded that he make music. He undertook to turn Aesop into poetry in order to be on the safe side. Yet, he did not doubt that the end of his effort was the quest for the good. La Fontaine's denial that music makes men good both qualifies the degree of his inspiration from Socrates and seems to vindicate Rousseau. Note, however, what La Fontaine said of fables in his own name:

> deux points; inventions utiles et agréables: ce sont eux qui ont introduit les sciences parmi les hommes. Ésope a trouvé un art singulier de les joindre l'un avec l'autre.

La Fontaine finds an ancient source for the modern focus on the useful and agreeable or pleasant. In his version, however, those are the sources, not of moral sentiments but, of sciences! Hume's view seems therefore an inversion, insofar as it has any roots in this tradition. La Fontaine was still more explicit:

> Et comme, par définition du point, de la ligne, de la surface, et par d'autres principes trés familiers, nous parvenons a des connaissances qui mésurent enfin le ciel et la terre, de même aussi, par les raisonnements et conséquences que l'on peut tirer de ces fables, on se forme le jugement et les mœurs, on se rend capable de grandes choses.[17]

Presumably, fables which do not "make man better" but which nevertheless "make one capable of great things" in the same way that science enables one to measure great things leave the choice of what one is to do in one's own hands. They "shape" without forming judgment. That would mean that judgment is formed by views of the useful and the pleasant. Thus, fables as a method of instruction—in Hume's view, no more powerful than philosophy itself on moral questions in the modern era—may convey rational guidance for moral choice only to the extent that rational guidance for moral choice remains possible on the basis of the useful and the pleasant. La Fontaine, in other words, did not go so far as Rousseau thought he had to go, but nevertheless left it as questionable whether there remained any guidance for human beings as to ends. The task of

Temple de Gnide seems immense beyond expectation; neither Montesquieu's forerunners nor his successors (save perhaps for Socrates and his students) point to the marriage of law and reason as a reasonable enterprise.

Le Temple de Gnide: The Text

> *. . . Neither your murmuring doves,*
> *nor ivied branches, nor the conquering trumpet's mouth.*
> Fragment of an *epithalamium* by Emperor Gallienus

The Translator's Preface*

A French ambassador to the Turkish court, known for his taste for the belles-lettres and having purchased several Greek manuscripts, brought them into France. A few of these manuscripts having fallen into my hands, I found among them the work of which I here offer a translation.

Very little of Greek authors has survived to our time, either because their works were destroyed in the ruining of libraries or because of the negligence of the families which possessed them.

From time to time we will recover some morsels of these treasure troves. They have even found some works in the very tombs of the authors themselves, and—what is very nearly the same thing—this present work was discovered among the books of a Greek bishop.

We know neither the name of the author nor the time in which he lived. All that can be said of him is that he was not earlier than Sappho since he speaks of her in his work.

With respect to my translation, it is faithful. I have avoided any elegances which were not in my author as not elegant at all. And frequently have I avoided the less lively expression in order the better to appropriate that which renders his thought.

I have been encouraged to make this translation by the success which that of Tasso[18] has had. He who translated that one will not take it unkindly that I am following the same path as he. He has distinguished himself in the business in such a manner as to fear nothing even from them in whom he has the most inspired imitation.

---

* By Charles de Secondat, Baron de La Brede et de Montesquieu. Montesquieu affects to have discovered the document and to serve only as a translator. Interestingly, the epigram seems excluded from this claim.

Le Temple de Gnide: **The Text**

. . . Non murmura vestra columbae,
Brachia non hederae, non vincant oscula conchae.
fragment d'un *epithalame* de l'emperor Gallien

Préface du Traducteur

Un ambassadeur de France à la Porte ottomane, connu par son goût pour les lettres, ayant acheté plusieurs manuscrits grecs, il les porta en France. Quelques uns de ces manuscrits m'étant tombés entre les mains; j'y ai trouvé l'ouvrage dont je donne ici la traduction.

Peu d'auteurs grecs sont venus jusqu'à nous, soit qu'ils aient péri dans la ruine des bibliothèques, ou par la négligence des familles qui les possédoient.

Nous recouvrons de temps en temps quelques pièces de ces trésors. On a trouvé des ouvrages jusque dans les tombeaux de leurs auteurs; et, ce qui est à peu près la même chose, on a trouvé celui-ci parmi les livres d'un évêque grec.

On ne sait ni le nom de l'auteur, ni le temps auquel il a vécu. Tout ce qu'on en peut dire, c'est qu'il n'est pas antérieur à Sapho, puisqu'il en parle dans son ouvrage.

Quant à ma traduction, elle est fidèle. J'ai cru que les beautés qui n'étoient point dans mon auteur, n'étoient point des beautés: et j'ai souvent quitté l'expression la moins vive, pour prendre celle qui rendoit mieux sa pensée.

J'ai été encouragé à cette traduction par le succès qu'a eu celle du Tasse. Celui qui l'a faite ne trouvera pas mauvais que je coure la même carrière que lui. Il s'y est distingué d'une manière à ne rien craindre de ceux même à qui il a donné le plus d'émulation.

This little novel is a sort of canvas upon which someone has deliberately painted the most agreeable objects. The public has found laughable ideas in this: a certain grandioseness in descriptions and naivete in feelings.

There is to be found here an original character which has caused the critics to wonder what was its model. That is very high praise when the work is not otherwise scorned.

Some intellectuals have not recognized in this that which they call art. But if the work has given pleasure, you must see that the heart has not shown to them all its rules.

A man who bothers to translate will not patiently endure that others should not think so highly of his author as he himself does. Thus, I admit that those *messieurs* have angered me furiously. Still, I beg of them to allow the young to judge of a book which—no matter what the language in which it was written—was certainly written for them. I beg the wise gentlemen not to disturb the young in their deciding. Only very well curled and powdered heads could understand wholly the merit of the *Temple de Gnide*.

With respect to the gentler sex, to which I owe the few happy moments I may count in my life, I wish with all my heart that this work might be pleasing to them. I still worship them. And, if they are no longer the object of my attentions, they remain at least the object of my longings.

But if serious men should insist upon a less frivolous work from me, I am able to satisfy them. For more than thirty years I've been working on a book of a dozen pages, which must contain all that which we know about metaphysics, politics, and ethics, and everything which some great authors have neglected in the volumes which they have offered on these very sciences.

First Chant

Venus prefers her residence at Cnidus to those of Paphos and Amathus.[19] She does not come down from Olympus without stopping by the Cnidians. So much has she accustomed the people of Cnidus to seeing her that they no longer feel that sacred awe which the presence of a god inspires. Occasionally she conceals herself with a cloud, but they recognize her from the divine odor which her ambrosia-perfumed hair gives off.

Ce petit roman est une espèce de tableau où l'on a peint, avec choix, les objets les plus agréables. Le public y a trouvé des idées riantes, une certaine magnificence dans les descriptions, et de la naïveté dans les sentiments.

Il y a trouvé un caractère original, qui a fait demander aux critiques quel en étoit le modèle: ce qui devient un grand éloge, lorsque l'ouvrage n'est pas méprisable d'ailleurs.

Quelques sçavans n'y ont point reconnu ce qu'ils appellent l'art. Il n'est point, disent-ils, selon les règles. Mais si l'ouvrage a plu, vous verrez que le cœur ne leur a pas dit toutes les règles.

Un homme qui se mêle de traduire, ne souffre point patiemment que l'on n'estime pas son auteur autant qu'il le fait; et j'avoue que ces messieurs m'ont mis dans une furieuse colère: mais je les prie de laisser les jeunes gens juger d'un livre qui, en quelque langue qu'il ait été écrit, a certainement été fait pour eux. Je les prie de ne point les troubler dans leurs décisions. Il n'y a que des têtes bien frisées et bien poudrées qui connoissent tout le mérite du *Temple de Gnide*.

A l'égard du beau sexe, à qui je dois le peu de moments heureux que je puis compter dans ma vie, je souhaite de tout mon cœur que cet ouvrage puisse lui plaire. Je l'adore encore; et, s'il n'est plus l'objet de mes occupations, il l'est de mes regrets.

Que si les gens graves désiraient de moi quelque ouvrage moins frivole, je suis en état de les satisfaire. Il y a trente ans que je travaille à un livre de douze pages, qui doit contenir tout ce que nous sçavons sur la métaphysique, la politique et la morale, et tout ce que de grands auteurs ont oublié dans les volumes qu'ils ont donnés sur ces sciences-là.

Chant Premier

Vénus préfère le séjour de Gnide à celui de Paphos et d'Amathonte. Elle ne descend point de l'Olympe sans venir parmi les Gnidiens. Elle a tellement accoutumé ce peuple heureux à sa vue, qu'il ne sent plus cette horreur sacrée qu'inspire la présence des dieux. Quelquefois elle se couvre d'un nuage, & on la reconnoît à l'odeur divine qui sort de ses cheveux parfumés d'ambroisie.

The town is in the middle of countryside over which the gods have poured benefactions with generous hands. People there profit from an eternal springtime; the soil, happily fertile, provides every wish; numberless flocks graze around there; and the winds seem to rule only to the extent of spreading everywhere the spirit of flowers. Birds sing ceaselessly. You would say that the woods ring with harmony. Brooks murmur down into the plains. A sweet warmth causes everything to blossom, and the air itself only betokens deep pleasure.

Near the town stands the palace of Venus. Vulcan had even constructed its foundations himself; he worked for his adultress whenever he wished to make her forget the cruel insult he made of her before the gods.

It would be impossible for me to offer an idea of the charms of that palace. Only the Graces would be able to describe the things that they have done. Gold, azure, rubies, and diamonds sparkle there throughout . . . but I'm painting the riches and not the beauties.

Its gardens are enchanted: Flora and Pomona have tended them; their nymphs cultivated them. Fruit there multiplies in the hand which picks it; flowers replace the fruit. When Venus promenades in her gardens, surrounded by Cnidians, one would think that they were going to ruin those delightful gardens in their wildly happy games, but by some hidden art everything is instantly repaired.

Venus loves to see the naive dances of the Cnidian girls. Her nymphs mix with them. The goddess joins in their games. Throwing off her majesty and sitting among them, she sees joy and innocence reign in their hearts.

One notices a great prairie far away, brimful with the colors of flowers. A shepherd and his lady were picking them, and the flower that she chose was always the most beautiful. He believed that Flora had made it especially. The river Cephis watered that prairie, twisting and turning through it a thousand times. It stopped wandering shepherdesses and required the sweet kisses they promised.

La ville est au milieu d'une contrée sur laquelle les dieux ont versé leurs bienfaits à pleines mains; on y jouit d'un printemps éternel; la terre, heureusement fertile, y prévient tous les souhaits; les troupeaux paissent sans nombre; les vents semblent n'y régner que pour répandre partout l'esprit des fleurs; les oiseaux y chantent sans cesse; vous diriez que les bois sont harmonieux; les ruisseaux murmurent dans les plaines; une chaleur douce fait tout éclore; l'air ne s'y respire qu'avec la volupté.

Auprès de la ville, est le palais de Vénus; Vulcain lui-même en a bâti les fondements; il travailla pour son infidèle, quand il voulut lui faire oublier le cruel affront qu'il lui fit devant les dieux.

Il me serait impossible de donner une idée des charmes de ce palais; il n'y a que les Grâces qui puissent décrire les choses qu'elles ont faites. L'or, l'azur, les rubis, les diamans y brillent de toutes parts . . . Mais j'en peins les richesses, & non pas les beautés.

Les jardins en sont enchantés: Flore et Pomone en ont pris soin; leurs nymphes les cultivent. Les fruits y renaissent sous la main qui les cueille; les fleurs succèdent aux fruits. Quand Vénus s'y promène, entourée de ses Gnidiennes, vous diriez que, dans leurs jeux folâtres, elles vont détruire ces jardins délicieux: mais, par une vertu secrète, tout se répare en un instant.

Vénus aime à voir les danses naïves des filles de Gnide. Ses nymphes se confondent avec elles. La déesse prend part à leurs jeux; elle se dépouille de sa majesté; assise au milieu d'elles, elle voit régner dans leurs cœurs la joie & l'innocence.

On découvre de loin une grande prairie, toute parée de l'émail des fleurs. Le berger vient les cueillir avec sa bergère; mais celle qu'elle a trouvée est toujours la plus belle, & il croit que Flore l'a faite exprès. Le fleuve Céphée arrose cette prairie, & y fait mille détours. Il arrête les bergères fugitives: il faut qu'elles donnent le tendre baiser qu'elles avoient promis.

When nymphs approached the river's bank, it stopped in its course. Its waves, which rolled in, come up against others which no longer rolled. But when they bathe themselves the waters are perfectly amorous. They turn all about the nymphs, sometimes rising up in order to embrace them the better. The river lifts the nymph; it runs away; it carries her with it. Her timid companions think to cry, but the river has borne the nymph on its waves. Charmed by its so dear burden, it promenades her on a liquid plain. Ultimately, regretting to release her, it slowly escorts her to its bank and consoles her companions.

Next the prairie is a stand of myrtles in which paths make a thousand turnings. Lovers repair there to relate their heartaches to one another. Eros, who amuses them, always leads them through the most secret paths.

Not far away is an old, holy woods into which hardly a glimpse of daylight penetrates. Oak trees which seem immortal incline their unperceived heads towards heaven. One feels in this woods a religious terror and might believe that this was the home of the gods when men had not yet emerged from the earth.

Upon re-discovering daylight one climbs a small hill upon which stands the temple of Venus. There is nothing in the world holier or more sacred than that spot.

In this temple did Venus see Adonis for the first time. Poison ran through the goddess's heart. "What?" she demanded. "Could I love a mortal? Alas! I feel that I adore him. Let no one any longer make vows to me; in Cnidus there is no longer any god but Adonis."

It was here that Venus summoned the Erotica when, stung by a bold rejection, she consulted them. She did not know whether she should expose her naked self to the Trojan shepherd's view. She arranged her cestus hidden beneath her hair, perfumed by her nymphs, and climbed into a chariot drawn by swans. Venus entered Phrygia. The shepherd wavered between Juno and Pallas. He saw Venus. His eyes wandered and failed. The golden apple dropped at the feet of the goddess. Adonis wanted to speak; his confusion determined his fate.

To this temple came young Psyche with her mother, and Eros [Cupid], flying about the golden columns, was himself surprised by one look from her. He felt all the miseries that he had made others suffer. "So this," he said, "is how I injure them! I can neither bear my bow nor my arrows." He fell at Psyche's breast. "Ah! I," said he, "I begin to sense that I am the pleasure god."

Lorsque les nymphes approchent de ses bords, il s'arrête, & ses flots, qui fuyoient, trouvent des flots qui ne fuient plus. Mais, lorsqu'une d'elles se baigne, il est plus amoureux encore; ses eaux tournent autour d'elle; quelquefois il se soulève pour l'embrasser mieux; il l'enlève, il fuit, il l'entraîne. Ses compagnes timides commencent à pleurer: mais il la soutient sur ses flots, &, charmé d'un fardeau si cher, il la promène sur sa plaine liquide; enfin, désespéré de la quitter, il la porte lentement sur le rivage, et console ses compagnes.

A côté de la prairie, est un bois de myrtes dont les routes font mille détours. Les amans y viennent se conter leurs peines: l'Amour, qui les amuse, les conduit par des routes toujours plus secrettes.

Non loin de là est un bois antique & sacré, où le jour n'entre qu'à peine: des chênes, qui semblent immortels, portent au ciel une tête qui se dérobe aux deux. On y sent une frayeur religieuse: vous diriez que c'était la demeure des dieux, lorsque les hommes n'étaient pas encore sortis de la terre.

Quand on a trouvé la lumière du jour, on monte une petite colline, sur laquelle est le temple de Vénus: l'univers n'a rien de plus saint ni de plus sacré que ce lieu.

Ce-fut dans ce temps que Vénus vit pour la première fois Adonis: le poison coula au cœur de la déesse. Quoi! dit-elle, j'aimerois un mortel! Hélas! je sens que je l'adore. Qu'on ne m'adresse plus dé vœux: il n'y a plus à Gnide d'autre dieu qu'Adonis.

Ce fut dans ce lieu qu'elle appela les Amours, lorsque, piquée d'un défi téméraire, elle les consulta. Elle étoit en doute si elle s'exposeroit nue aux regards du berger troyen. Elle cacha sa ceinture sous ses cheveux; ses nymphes la parfumèrent; elle monta sur son char traîné par des cygnes, & arriva dans la Phrygie. Le berger balançoit entre Junon et Palles; il la vit, et ses regards errèrent et moururent: la pomme d'or tomba aux pieds de la déesse: il voulut parler, & son désordre décida.

Ce fut dans ce temple que la jeune Psyché vint avec sa mère, lorsque l'Amour, qui voloit autour des lambris dorés, fut surpris lui-même par un de ses regards. Il sentit tous les maux qu'il fait souffrir: C'est ainsi, dit-il, que je blesse! Je ne puis soutenir mon arc ni mes flèches. Il tomba sur le sein de Psyché. Ah! dit-il, je commence à sentir que je suis le dieu des plaisirs.

Upon entering this temple one feels a secret charm in one's heart that is impossible to describe. The soul is seized by those raptures which the gods themselves only feel upon entering their celestial abode.

Every smiling aspect of nature is joined to all that art has been able to conceive of the noblest and worthiest of the gods.

A single hand, immortal doubtless, has adorned the temple throughout with paintings which seem to breathe. One gazes upon the birth of Venus, the ecstasy of the gods who beheld her, her own shame upon seeing herself naked, and that modesty which is the earliest of graces.

There one sees the loves of Mars and the goddess. The painter represented the god in his chariot, proud and fierce indeed. Fame flew all about him; Fear and Death marched ahead of his sweat-soaked coursers. He is joining in the melee and a thick dust begins to cover him. On another side Mars is seen languidly lying in a bed of roses, smiling upon Venus. You wouldn't recognize him but for a few godly characteristics which remain. The Pleasure Muses make garlands and with them tie the two lovers. Their eyes seem to run together. They sigh and, attentive only to each other, take no notice of the Erotica gamboling about them.

In a separate apartment the painter has portrayed the wedding rites of Venus and Vulcan. The entire heavenly court was gathered together. The god appeared less somber but also less thoughtful than usual. The goddess coldly surveyed the communal joy. Negligently, she offered him her hand, which seemed to disappear in his. She withdrew from him her eyes which barely reached him and turned towards the Graces.

In another painting one sees Juno making the marriage ceremony. Venus accepts the cup in order to swear eternal fidelity to Vulcan: the gods smile; and Vulcan listens to her with pleasure.

From the other side one sees the impatient god carrying off his divine bride: she offers so much resistance that one would imagine that this was Ceres' daughter whom Pluto was going to ravish, if the eye which beheld Venus could ever betray itself.

Further on from there one sees him take her up to bear her away to the nuptial couch. A mob of gods follow them. The goddess questions herself, and wants to escape from the arms which hold her. Her dress draws back from her knees, the veil flies about, but Vulcan repairs the beautiful disarray, more careful to cover her than to ravish her.

Lorsqu'on entre dans ce temple, on sent dans le cœur un charme secret qu'il est impossible d'exprimer: l'âme est saisie de ces ravissements que les dieux ne sentent eux-mêmes que lorsqu'ils sont dans la demeure céleste.

Tout ce que la nature a de riant est joint à tout ce que l'art a pu imaginer de plus noble & de plus digne des dieux.

Une main, sans doute immortelle, l'a partout orné de peintures qui semblent respirer. On y voit la naissance de Vénus; le ravissement des dieux qui la virent; son embarras de se voir toute nue; & cette pudeur qui est la première des grâces.

On y voit lés amours de Mars et de la déesse. Le peintre a représenté le dieu sur son char, fier & même terrible: la Renommée vole autour de lui; la Peur et la Mort marchent devant ses coursiers couverts d'écume; il entre dans la mêlée, & une poussière épaisse commence à le dérober. D'un autre côté, on le voit couché languissamment sur un lit de roses; il sourit à Vénus: vous ne le reconnoissez qu'à quelques traits divins qui restent encore. Les Plaisirs font des guirlandes dont ils lient les deux amants: leurs yeux semblent se confondre; ils soupirent; &, attentifs l'un à l'autre, ils ne regardent pas les Amours qui se jouent autour d'eux.

Il y a un appartement séparé, où le peintre a représenté les noces de Vénus et de Vulcain: toute la cour céleste y est assemblée. Le dieu paroît moins sombre, mais aussi pensif qu'à l'ordinaire. La déesse regarde d'un air froid la joie commune; elle lui donne négligemment une main, qui semble se dérober; elle retire de dessus lui des regards qui portent à peine; et se tourne du côté des Grâces.

Dans un autre tableau, on voit Junon qui fait la cérémonie du mariage. Vénus prend la coupe, pour jurer à Vulcain une fidélité éternelle: les dieux sourient; & Vulcain l'écoute avec plaisir.

De l'autre côté, on voit le dieu impatient, qui entraîne sa divine épouse; elle fait tant de résistance, que l'on croiroit que c'est la fille de Cérès que Pluton va ravir, si L'œil qui voit Vénus pouvoit jamais se tromper.

Plus loin de là, on le voit qui l'enlève, pour l'emporter sur le lit nuptial. Les dieux suivent en foule. La déesse se débat, et veut échapper des bras qui la tiennent. Sa robe fuit ses genoux, la toile vole: mais Vulcain répare ce beau désordre, plus attentif à la cacher qu'ardent à la ravir.

Finally, one sees him lay her upon the couch that Hymen had arranged. He encloses her within the drapes, and he imagines to hold her there for ever. The importunate attendants withdraw, and he is pleased to see them move away. The goddesses gambol among themselves, but the gods seem sad. And the sadness of Mars suggests something as cloudy as dark jealousy.

Pleased by the magnificence of her temple, the goddess herself wished to set up her cult there. She established its ceremonies, instituted its celebrations. There, she is one and the same time divinity and priestess.

The worship offered to her in the greater part of the earth is more of a profanation than a religion. She has some temples in which all the young maidens of the town prostitute themselves in her honor, and provide themselves a dowry by their devotion. She has other temples in which each married woman undertakes, one time in her life, to surrender herself to anyone who might choose her, and to cast into the sanctuary the money she receives. There are still other temples to which courtisans, more highly honored than matrons, bear their offerings. Still others exist, finally, where the men are eunuchs and dress themselves like women in order to function within the sanctuary, consecrating to the goddess both the sex they no longer have and that which they can not have.

But she wanted the Cnidian people to have a purer worship and to offer up honors more worthy of the goddess. In that place sighs are sacrifices and a tender heart is an offering. Each lover presents his vows to his mistress, and Venus accepts them on her behalf.

Wherever beauty is people adore it as Venus herself. For beauty is as divine as Venus.

Hearts inflamed with love enter the temple. They approach and embrace the altars of faithfulness and constancy.

Men burdened by the stringencies of a cruel lady enter therein to sigh; they sense their torment diminishing and discover in their hearts that flatterer, hope.

The goddess, who promised happiness to true lovers, always proportions it to their sufferings.

Jealousy is a passion which one may have, but he is obliged to silence her. One secretly loves the caprices of his mistress, just as one loves the gods' decrees, which become more exact whenever one dares to complain of them.

Enfin, on le voit qui vient de la poser sur le lit que l'Hymen a préparé: il l'enferme dans les rideaux; & il croit l'y tenir pour jamais. La troupe importune se retire: il est charmé de la voir s'éloigner. Les déesses jouent entre elles; mais les dieux paraissent tristes; & la tristesse de Mars a quelque chose d'aussi sombre que la noire jalousie.

Charmée de la magnificence de son temple, la déesse elle-même y a voulu établir son culte: elle en a réglé les cérémonies, institué les fêtes; & elle y est, en même temps, la divinité & la prêtresse.

Le culte qu'on lui rend presque par toute la terre, est plutôt une profanation qu'une religion. Elle a des temples où toutes les filles de la ville se prostituent en son honneur, & se font une dot des profits de leur dévotion. Elle en a où chaque femme mariée va, une fois en sa vie, se donner à celui qui la choisit, et jette dans le sanctuaire l'argent qu'elle a reçu. Il y en a d'autres où les courtisanes de tous les pays, plus honorées que les matrones, vont porter leurs offrandes. Il y en a, enfin, où les hommes se font eunuques, et s'habillent en femmes pour servir dans le sanctuaire, consacrant à la déesse, & le sexe qu'ils n'ont plus, & celui qu'ils ne peuvent pas avoir.

Mais elle a voulu que le peuple de Gnide eût un culte plus pur, & lui rendît des honneurs plus dignes d'elle. Là, les sacrifices sont des soupirs, et les offrandes un cœur tendre. Chaque amant adresse ses vœux à sa maîtresse, et Vénus les reçoit pour elle.

Partout où se trouve la beauté, on l'adore comme Vénus même: car la beauté est aussi divine qu'elle.

Les cœurs amoureux viennent dans le temple; ils vont embrasser les autels de la Fidélité et de la Constance.

Ceux qui sont accablés des rigueurs d'une cruelle, y viennent soupirer; ils sentent diminuer leurs tourments; ils trouvent dans leur cœur la flatteuse espérance.

La déesse, qui a promis de faire le bonheur des vrais amans, le mesure toujours à leurs peines.

La jalousie est une passion qu'on peut avoir, mais qu'on doit taire. On adore en secret les caprices de sa maîtresse, comme on adore les décrets des dieux, qui deviennent plus justes lorsqu'on ose s'en plaindre.

Among divine benefactions are fire, the emotions of love, and even fury (anger). For to the very degree one is not master of his own heart, just so much is he more the master of the goddess.

Whoever has not surrendered his heart is profane; such enter not into the temple. From far away do they address vows to the goddess and implore her to deliver them from this freedom, which is only a power-lessness to form desires.

The goddess inspires young maidens with modesty—that charming quality places a new price on all the treasures they still hide.

But in these precincts young maidens have never blushed for a sincere passion, a naive feeling, or a tender avowal.

The heart always establishes the point at which it will surrender itself, but it is profane to give oneself without love.

Cupid oversees the happiness of the Cnidians. He selects the arrows with which he wounds them. When he sees a maiden afflicted with love, burdened by the stringencies of her beloved, he draws an arrow soaked in the waters of the river Oblivion. When he sees two lovers who begin to love another, he ceaselessly aims new arrows at them. When he sees one in whom love weakens, he makes it suddenly rejuvenate, or die. For he always spares the last days of languishing passion. One does not have to experience disgust before ceasing to love; greater sweetnesses cause him to forget lesser ones.

Cupid has removed from his quiver the cruel arrows with which he wounded Phedrus and Ariane, arrows mixed with love and hate and which served to display his power in the way that lightning reveals Jupiter's empire.

To the degree the god gives men the pleasure of loving, Venus attaches to it the happiness of pleasing.

Young maidens every day go into the sanctuary in order to perform their prayers to Venus. There they express some feelings as naive as the heart which gives birth to them. "Queen of Amathus," said one, "my flame for Thyrsis has died. I don't pray you to give me my love; just cause Ixiphilus to love me."

Another said in a low voice, "Powerfull goddess, give me the strength to hide somewhat my love from my shepherd, so that I may increase the value of the avowal of my love that I want to make to him."

"Cytherean goddess," said another, "I'm looking for solitude. The games of my comrades no longer please me. Maybe I'm in love. Ah! If I love someone, it can only be Daphnis."

On met au rang des faveurs divines le feu, les transports de l'amour et la fureur même: car, moins on est maître de son cœur, plus il est à la déesse.

Ceux qui n'ont point donné leur cœur sont des profanes, qui ne peuvent pas entrer dans le temple: ils adressent de loin leurs vœux à la déesse, et lui demandent de les délivrer de cette liberté, qui n'est qu'une impuissance de former des désirs.

La déesse inspire aux filles de la modestie cette qualité charmante donne un nouveau prix à tous les trésors qu'elle cache.

Mais jamais, dans ces lieux fortunés, elles n'ont rougi d'une passion sincère, d'un sentiment naïf, d'un aveu tendre.

Le cœur fixe toujours lui-même le moment auquel il doit se rendre: mais c'est une profanation de se rendre sans aimer.

L'Amour est attentif à la félicité des Gnidiens; il choisit les traits dont il les blesse. Lorsqu'il voit une amante affligée, accablée des rigueurs d'un amant, il prend une flèche trempée dans les eaux du fleuve d'Oubli. Quand il voit deux amants qui commencent à s'aimer, il tire sans cesse sur eux de nouveaux traits. Quand il en voit dont l'amour s'affoiblit, il le fait soudain renaître ou mourir: car il épargne toujours les derniers jours d'une passion languissante: on ne passe point par les dégoûts avant de cesser d'aimer; mais de plus grandes douceurs font oublier les moindres.

L'Amour a ôté de son carquois les traits cruels dont il blessa Phèdre et Ariane, qui, mêlés d'amour et de haine, servent à montrer sa puissance, comme la foudre sert à faire connaître l'empire de Jupiter.

A mesure que le dieu donne le plaisir d'aimer, Vénus y joint le bonheur de plaire.

Les filles entrent chaque jour dans le sanctuaire, pour faire leur prière à Vénus. Elles y expriment des sentiments naïfs comme le cœur qui les fait naître. Reine d'Amathonte, disoit une d'elles, ma flamme pour Thirsis est éteinte; je ne te demande pas de me rendre mon amour; fais seulement qu'Ixiphile m'aime.

Une autre disoit tout bas: Puissante déesse, donne moi la force de cacher quelque temps mon amour à mon berger, pour augmenter le prix de l'aveu que je veux lui en faire.

Déesse de Cythère, disait une autre, je cherche la solitude; les jeux de mes compagnes ne me plaisent plus. J'aime peut-être. Ah! si j'aime quelqu'un, ce ne peut être que Daphnis.

On holy days the maidens and young men arrive to recite hymns in Venus' honor. Often, they sing her glory by singing of their loves.

A young Cnidian, holding his mistress by the hand, sang as follows: "Cupid, when you saw Psyche you doubtlessly wounded her with the same arrows with which you now pierce my heart. Your happiness differed not from mine, because you sensed my fires and I have felt your pleasures."

I have seen all that I described. I have been to Cnidus. I saw Themira there, and I loved her. I've seen her again, and I loved her even more. I will spend the rest of my life at Cnidus with her, and I'll be the happiest of mortals.

We will go into the temple, and never will there have been a lover more faithful than I to enter there. We will go into Venus's palace and I will think it Themira's palace. I'll go into the countryside and pick flowers that I shall place upon her breast. Maybe I can lead her into the woods, where the paths become confused, and when she's lost, . . . Cupid, who inspires me, won't permit me to reveal his mysteries.

Second Chant

There is a holy cave at Cnidus, in which the nymphs live, where the goddess gives her oracles. The soil does not groan under footsteps. Hair doesn't stand on end. There are no priestesses as at Delphi, where Apollo motivates the Pythean. But Venus herself listens to mortals without playing false with their hopes and fears.

A flirt from the isle of Crete had come to Cnidus. She walked about surrounded by all the youths of Cnidus. She smiled at one, whispered to another, posed her arm in that of a third, and called after two others to follow her. She was beautiful and had been made up with skill. The tone of her voice was as phony as her eyes. O! Heavens! such frights she caused for true lovers! She presented herself to the oracle, as proud as the goddesses. But all of a sudden we heard a voice emanating from the sanctuary: "Persida, how dare you to bring your deceptions into the precincts where I reign with candor? I am going to punish you in a cruel way: I will take away your charms, but I shall leave your heart just as it is. You will summon every man that you will see; they will run from you as from a troublesome shadow. You will die haunted by scorn and rejection."

Dans les jours de fête, les filles & les jeunes garçons viennent réciter des hymnes en l'honneur dé Vénus: souvent ils chantent sa gloire, en chantant leurs amours.

Un jeune Gnidien, qui tenoit pas la main sa maîtresse, chantoit ainsi: Amour, lorsque tu vis Psyché, tu te blessas sans doute des mêmes traits dont tu viens de blesser mon cœur: ton bonheur n'étoit pas différent du mien; car tu sentais mes feux, & moi, j'ai senti tes plaisirs.

J'ai vu tout ce que je décris. J'ai été à Gnide; j'y ai vu Thémire, & je l'ai aimée: je l'ai vue encore, et je l'ai aimée davantage. Je resterai toute ma vie à Gnide avec elle; & je serai le plus heureux des mortels.

Nous irons dans le temple; & jamais il n'y sera entré un amant si fidèle: nous irons dans le palais de Vénus; et je croirai que c'est le palais de Thémire: j'irai dans la prairie, et je cueillerai des fleurs, que je mettrai sur son sein; peut-être que je pourrai la conduire dans le bocage, où tant de routes vont se confondre; et quand elle sera égarée, . . . L'Amour, qui m'inspire, me défend de révéler ses mystères.

Chant Second

II y a à Gnide un antre sacré que les nymphes habitent, où la déesse rend ses oracles. La terre ne mugit point sous les pieds; les cheveux ne se dressent point sur la tête; il n'y a point de prêtresse, comme à Delphes, où Apollon agite la Pythie: mais Vénus elle-même écoute les mortels, sans se jouer de leurs espérances, ni de leurs craintes.

Une coquette de l'île de Crète étoit venue à Gnide: elle marchait entourée de tous les jeunes Gnidiens: elle souriait à l'un, parlait à l'oreille à l'autre, soutenait son bras sur un troisième, criait à deux autres de la suivre. Elle était belle & parée avec art; le son de sa voix était imposteur comme ses yeux. O Ciel! que d'allarmes ne causa-t-elle point aux vraies amantes! Elle se présenta à l'oracle, aussi fière que les déesses: mais soudain nous entendîmes une voix qui sortait du sanctuaire: Perfide, comment oses-tu porter tes artifices jusque dans les lieux où je règne avec la candeur? Je vais te punir d'une manière cruelle: je t'ôterai tes charmes; mais je te laisserai le cœur comme il est. Tu appelleras tous les hommes que tu verras, ils te fuiront comme une ombre plaintive; & tu mourras accablée de refus & de mépris.

Next came a courtesan from Nocris, glittering in the spoils of her lovers. "Leave," said the goddess. "You are wrong if you believe that you can be the glory of my court. Your beauty shows that there are pleasures, but it does not offer them. Your heart is like steel, and even if you should see my son you could not be moved to love him. Go spread your favors among the cowardly men who seek them and who become disgusted with them. Go reveal to them those charms that one sees right away but that one loses forever. You are suited only to belittle my power."

A while later there came a rich man, the King of Lydia's tribute collector. "You seek of me," said the goddess, "something that I should not know how to do even though I am the goddess of love. You buy beautiful things in order to love them. But you don't love them, because you've purchased them. Your wealth will be useless to you, it will serve only to make you disgusted with all that is most charming in nature."

A young man from Doris, named Aristeus, came forth next. He had seen the lovely Camille in Cnidus and had fallen madly in love with her. He sensed completely the excess of his love, and he sought of Venus that he might be able to love Camille still more.

"I know your heart," the goddess told him. "You know how to love. I have found Camille worthy of you. I could have given her to the world's greatest king, but kings deserve her less than shepherds do."

Next, I appeared with Themira. The goddess said to me, "There is no mortal in my empire who yields me greater submission than you. But what do you wish that I might do? I neither know how to make you more in love, nor Themira more lovely." "Ah," I said to her, "great goddess, I've a thousand favors to request of you. Cause Themira to think only of me, to see only me. Cause her to awaken dreaming about me. Cause her to fear losing me, when I'm present, to long for me when I'm gone. Make it so that, always delighted to see me, she should nonetheless still feel sorry for every moment she has spent without me."

Third Chant

There are at Cnidus holy games which re-occur every year. Women arrive from everywhere to contest the prize for beauty. Then, shepherd girls are confused with the daughters of kings. For beauty alone bears the staff of authority there. Venus herself presides. She decides without weighing the sides; she knows very well who the happy mortal is whom she has granted the greatest favors.

Une courtisane de Nocrétis vint ensuite, toute brillante des dépouilles de ses amants. Va, dit la déesse, tu te trompes, si tu crois faire la gloire de mon empire: ta beauté fait voir qu'il y a des plaisirs; mais elle ne les donne pas. Ton cœur est comme le fer; &, quand tu verrois mon fils même, tu ne sçaurois l'aimer. Va prodiguer tes faveurs aux hommes lâches qui les demandent & qui s'en dégoûtent; va leur montrer des charmes que l'on voit soudain, & que l'on perd pour toujours. Tu n'es propre qu'à faire mépriser ma puissance.

Quelque temps après vint un homme riche, qui levoit les tributs du roi de Lydie. Tu me demandes, dit la déesse, une chose que je ne sçaurois faire, quoique je sois la déesse de l'amour. Tu achètes des beautés, pour les aimer; mais tu ne les aime pas, parce que tu les achètes. Tes trésors ne te seront point inutiles; ils te serviront à te dégoûter de tout ce qu'il y a de plus charmant dans la nature.

Un jeune homme de Doride, nommé Aristée, se présenta ensuite: il avoit vu à Gnide la charmante Camille; il en étoit éperdument amoureux il sentoit tout l'excès de son amour; & il venoit demander à Vénus qu'il pût l'aimer davantage.

Je connois ton cœur, lui dit la déesse: tu sçais aimer. J'ai trouvé Camille digne de toi: j'aurais pu la donner au plus grand roi du monde; mais les rois la méritent moins que les bergers.

Je parus ensuite avec Thémire. La déesse me dit: il n'y a point, dans mon empire, de mortel qui me soit plus soumis que toi. Mais que veux-tu que je fasse? Je ne sçaurois te rendre plus amoureux, ni Thémire plus charmante. Ah! lui dis-je, grande déesse, j'ai mille grâces à vous demander: faites que Thémire ne pense qu'à moi; qu'elle ne voie que moi; qu'elle se réveille en songeant à moi; qu'elle craigne de me perdre, quand je suis présent; qu'elle m'espère dans mon absence; que, toujours charmée de me voir, elle regrette encore tous les moments qu'elle a passés sans moi.

Chant Troisième

Il y a à Gnide des jeux sacrés, qui se renouvellent tous les ans: les femmes y viennent, de toutes parts, disputer le prix de la beauté. Là, les bergères sont confondues avec les filles des rois; car la beauté seule y porte les marques de l'empire. Vénus y préside elle-même. Elle décide sans balancer; elle sçait bien quelle est la mortelle heureuse qu'elle a le plus favorisée.

Many times did Helen bear away the prize. She triumphed when Theseus raped her. She triumphed when she had been kidnapped by Priam's son. She triumphed again when the gods had returned her to Menelaus after ten years of longing. Thus, that prince in Venus' judgment beheld himself as happy a husband as Theseus and Paris had been happy lovers.

From Corinth there came thirty young Maidens, whose hair fell to their shoulders in great curls. Ten came from Salamis. They had as yet seen the course of the sun only thirteen times. Fifteen maidens came from the Isle of Lesbos, and they said, the one to the other, "I feel wholly entranced; there is no one so lovely as you. If Venus looks at you with my eyes, she will crown you amidst all the beautiful girls of the universe."

From Miletus came fifty women. Nothing equalled the whiteness of their complexions and the evenness of their features. All either revealed or promised a beautiful body. The gods who shaped them could not have made anything more worthy for them if they had tried rather to give them perfections than charms.

There were a hundred women come from the isle of Cyprus. "We have," said they, "spent our youth in Venus' temple. To her have we sacrificed our virginity, and even our modesty. We don't blush for our appeal; our manners—sometimes brash and always free—must give us the advantage over a modesty constantly in alarm."

I saw the young maidens from Sparta the superb. Their dress was open on the sides, up to the waist, in the most daring fashion. Still, they behaved as prudes and maintained that they violated modesty only for love of their fatherland.

Sea, famous for your many shipwrecks, you know how to guard precious deposits. You calmed yourself when the ship Argo bore the golden fleece over your liquid surface. And when fifty beautiful girls left Colchis and trusted in you, you cradled yourself beneath them.

Hélène remporta ce prix plusieurs fois; elle triompha lorsque Thésée l'eut ravie; elle triompha lorsqu'elle eut été enlevée par le fils de Priam; elle triompha enfin, lorsque les dieux l'eurent rendue à Ménélas, après dix ans d'espérance: ainsi ce prince, au jugement de Vénus même, se vit aussi heureux époux que Thésée et Pâris avoient été heureux amants.

Il vint trente filles de Corinthe, dont les cheveux tombaient à grosses boucles sur les épaules. Il en vint dix de Salamine, qui n'avaient encore vu que treize fois le course du soleil. Il en vint quinze de l'île de Lesbos; et elles se disaient l'une à l'autre: Je me sens tout émue; il n'y a rien de si charmant que vous: si Vénus vous voit des mêmes yeux que moi, elle vous couronnera au milieu de toutes les beautés de l'univers.

Il vint cinquante femmes de Milet. Rien n'approchoit de la blancheur de leur teint & de la régularité de leurs traits: tout faisoit voir ou promettoit un beau corps; et les dieux, qui les formèrent, n'auroient rien fait de plus digne d'eux, s'ils n'avoient plus cherché à leur donner des perfections que des grâces.

Il vint cent femmes de l'île de Chypre. Nous avons, disoient-elles, passé notre jeunesse dans le temple de Vénus; nous lui avons consacré notre virginité et notre pudeur même. Nous ne rougissons point de nos charmes: nos manières, quelquefois hardies & toujours libres, doivent nous donner de l'avantage sur une pudeur qui s'alarme sans cesse.

Je vis des filles de la superbe Lacédémone. Leur robe étoit ouverte par les côtés, depuis la ceinture, de la manière la plus immodeste: et cependant, elles faisoient les prudes, et soutenoient qu'elles ne violoient la pudeur que par amour pour la patrie.

Mer fameuse par tant de naufrages, vous sçavez conserver des dépôts précieux! Vous vous calmâtes, lorsque le navire Argo porta la toison d'or sur votre plaine liquide; &, lorsque cinquante beautés sont parties de Colchos, & se sont confiées à vous, vous vous êtes courbée sous elles.

I also saw Oriane, image of the goddesses. All the Lydian beauties encircled their queen. Ahead of herself she had sent one hundred girls who presented to Venus an offering of two hundred talents. Candaulus himself came, more distinguished by his love than his royal purple. His days and nights were passed devouring with his eyes Oriane's loveliness. His eyes wandered over her beautiful body and they never rested. "Alas!" said he, "I am happy. But that is a thing which is known only by Venus and me. My happiness would be greater if it could produce jealousy. Beautiful queen, abandon those vain ornamentations. Drop that troublesome linen and show yourself to the world. Forget the beauty prize! Demand an altar!"

Nearby there were twenty Babylonian women. They wore purple dresses embroidered with gold. They thought that their luxury would increase their value. There were some of them who, as proof of their beauty, wore the riches that their beauty had produced for them.

Further on I saw a hundred women from Egypt. They had black eyes and black hair. Their husbands were with them, and the men said, "The laws submit us to you in honor of Isis. But your beauty rules us more strongly than the laws. We obey you with the same pleasure one obeys gods. We are the happiest slaves in the world.

"Duty assures you of our fidelity, but only love can promise us yours.

"Be less sensitive to the glory you will acquire in Cnidus than to the homage that you are able to find in your home with a quiet husband who, while you busy yourself with outside business, must wait in the breast of the family for the heart you bring back to him."

There came some women from that powerful town which sends its vessels to the ends of the earth. Ornamentation weighted their superb heads. Every portion of the world seemed to have contributed to their decoration.

Ten beautiful girls came from climes where the day begins; they were daughters of the Dawn. In order to see her, they would get ahead of Dawn every day. They grumbled about the sun, who caused their mother to disappear. They complained about their mother, who revealed herself to them just like she did to every other mortal.

Je vis aussi Oriane, semblable aux déesses. Toutes les beautés de Lydie entouroient leur reine. Elle avoit envoyé devant elle cent jeunes filles, qui avoient présenté à Vénus une offrande de deux cents talents. Candaule étoit venu lui-même, plus distingué par son amour que par la pourpre royale: il passait les jours et les nuits à dévorer de ses regards les charmes d'Oriane: ses yeux erraient sur son beau corps, et ses yeux ne se lassaient jamais. Hélas! disait-il, je suis heureux; mais c'est une chose qui n'est sçue que de Vénus et de moi: mon bonheur seroit plus grand, s'il donnoit de l'envie! Belle reine, quittez ces vains ornements; faites tomber cette toile importune; montrez-vous à l'univers; laissez le prix· de la beauté, et demandez des autels.

Auprès de là étoient vingt Babyloniennes elles avoient des robes de pourpre brodées d'or; elles croyoient que leur luxe augmentoit leur prix. Il y en avoit qui portoient, pour preuve de leur beauté, les richesses qu'elle leur avoit fait acquérir.

Plus loin, je vis cent femmes d'Égypte, qui avoient les yeux & les cheveux noirs. Leurs maris étoient auprès d'elles, et ils disoient: Les lois nous soumettent à vous en l'honneur d'Isis, mais votre beauté a sur nous un empire plus fort que celui des lois; nous vous obéissons avec le même plaisir que l'on obéit aux dieux; nous sommes les plus heureux esclaves de l'univers.

Le devoir vous répond de notre fidélité; mais il n'y a que l'amour qui puisse nous promettre la vôtre.

Soyez moins sensibles à la gloire que vous acquerrez à Gnide, qu'aux hommages que vous pouvez trouver dans votre maison, auprès d'un mari tranquille, qui, pendant que vous vous occupez des affaires du dehors, doit attendre, dans le sein de votre famille, le cœur que vous lui rapportez.

Il vint des femmes de cette ville puissante qui envoie ses vaisseaux au bout de l'univers: les ornements fatiguoient leur tête superbe; toutes les parties du monde sembloient avoir contribué à leur parure.

Dix beautés vinrent des lieux où commence le jour: elles étoient filles de l'Aurore; et, pour la voir, elles se levoient tous les jours avant elle. Elles se plaignoient du Soleil, qui faisoit disparaître leur mère; elles se plaignoient de leur mère, qui ne se montroit à elles que comme au reste des mortels.

I also saw a queen of the people of India beneath a tent. She was encircled by her girls, who had already begun to long for their mother's charms. She was served by eunuchs whose eyes were fixed on the ground. Since they had breathed the air of Cnidus, they felt their frightful melancholy with double the force.

The women of Cadiz, who are at the ends of the earth, also competed for the prize. There is no country on earth where a beautiful woman would not receive homage. But only the greatest homages can appease the ambitions of a beautiful woman.

Next appeared the maidens of Cnidus. Beautiful without decorations, they wore charms instead of pearls and rubies. One saw on their heads only Flora's gifts, but they were more worthy of Zephyr's embrace. Their dresses had no other advantage than that they outlined lovely figures and had been woven by their own hands.

One did not see the young Camille among all those beauties. She had said, "I don't want to compete for the beauty prize; enough for me that my darling Aristeus thinks I'm beautiful."

Diana added celebrity to the competition by her presence. She did not come to compete, for goddesses don't compare themselves to mortals. I saw her alone. She was beautiful like Venus. I saw her next to Venus. She was no longer anything but Diana.

Never was there such a grand spectacular. The people were separated into peoples. The eye wandered from country to country, from sunset to dawn. Cnidus seemed to be the entire earth.

The gods distributed beauty among the nations as nature has distributed it among goddesses. There, one beheld Pallas' proud beauty; here, the grandeur and majesty of Juno; further on, the simplicity of Diana, the daintiness of Thetis, the loveliness of the Graces, and occasionally Venus' smile.

It seemed that every people had a specific manner of expressing modesty, and that all those women would want to flirt by their eyes. Some uncovered the throat, and hid the shoulder. Others revealed the shoulders and covered the throat. Those who hid their feet compensated you by some other delights. From elsewhere they blushed at that which, here, people call good manners.

The gods are so charmed by Themira, that they never look at her without smiling upon their creation. Of all the goddesses only Venus looks upon her with pleasure, and only the gods do not grumble from a little jealousy.

Je vis, sous une tente, une reine d'un peuple des Indes. Elle étoit entourée de ses filles, qui déjà faisoient espérer les charmes de leur mère des eunuques la servoient, et leurs yeux regardoient la terre; car, depuis qu'ils avoient respiré l'air de Gnide, ils avoient senti redoubler leur affreuse mélancolie.

Les femmes de Cadis, qui sont aux extrémités de la terre, disputèrent aussi le prix. Il n'y a point de pays dans l'univers, où une belle ne reçoive des hommages; mais il n'y a que les plus grands hommages qui puissent apaiser l'ambition d'une belle.

Les filles de Gnide parurent ensuite. Belles sans ornements, elles avoient des grâces, au lieu de perles et de rubis. On ne voyoit sur leur tête que les présents de Flore; mais ils y étoient plus dignes des embrassements de Zéphyr. Leur robe n'avoit d'autre mérite que celui de marquer une taille charmante, & d'avoir été filée de leurs propres mains.

Parmi toutes ces beautés, on ne vit point la jeune Camille. Elle avoit dit Je ne veux point disputer le prix de la beauté; il me suffit que mon cher Aristée me trouve belle.

Diane rendoit ces jeux célèbres par sa présence. Elle n'y venoit point disputer le prix: car les déesses ne se comparent point aux mortelles. Je la vis seule, elle étoit belle comme Vénus: je la vis auprès de Vénus, elle n'étoit plus que Diane.

Il n'y eut jamais un si grand spectacle: les peuples étoient séparés des peuples; les yeux erroient de pays en pays, depuis le couchant jusqu'à l'aurore: il sembloit que Gnide fût tout l'univers.

Les dieux ont partagé la beauté entre les nations, comme la nature l'a partagée entre les déesses. Là, on voyoit la beauté fière de Pallas; ici, la grandeur et la majesté de Junon; plus loin, la simplicité de Diane, la délicatesse de Thétis, le charme des Grâces, et quelquefois le sourire de Vénus.

Il sembloit que chaque peuple eût une manière particulière d'exprimer sa pudeur; & que toutes ces femmes voulussent se jouer des yeux: les unes découvroient la gorge, et cachoient leurs épaules; les autres montroient les épaules, et couvroient la gorge; celles qui vous déroboient le pied, vous payoient par d'autres charmes: et là on rougissoit, de ce qu'ici on appeloit bienséance.

Les dieux sont si charmés de Thémire, qu'ils ne la regardent jamais sans sourire de leur ouvrage. De toutes les déesses, il n'y a que Vénus qui la voie avec plaisir, et que les dieux ne raillent point d'un peu de jalousie.

As one notices a rose amidst the flowers growing in the weeds, one distinguishes Themira among so many beauties. They didn't have time to rival her; they were bested before they could fear her. From the moment she appeared Venus looked on no one else. She summoned the Graces. "Go crown her," she told them. "Of all the beautiful women I see, that one alone resembles you."

Fourth Chant

While Themira was busy with her companions, worshipping the goddess, I went into a secluded woods. There I found the gentle Aristeus. We had seen one another the day we went to consult the oracle. That was sufficient to engage us to be with one another. For Venus places in the heart, in the presence of an inhabitant of Cnidus, the secret charm which two friends discover when, after a long absence, they sense in their arms the sweet object of their concerns.

Enchanted with one another, we felt that we shared one heart. It seemed that affectionate friendship had fallen from heaven, in order to reside among us. We related thousands of things about our life. Here, just about, is what I said to him:

I was born in Sybaris, where Antilochus, my father, was Venus's bishop. In that town no one distinguishes between desires and needs. They banished every art which could disturb a tranquil somnolence. At public expense they give prizes to them that can discover the newest pleasures. The citizens never remember any but clowns who have diverted them, and they have forgotten the names of magistrates who have governed them.

There, men abuse the soil's fertility, which produces an eternal abundance. The gods' graces around Sybaris only encourage luxury and softness.

The men are so effeminate, their dress so like that of the women; they make up their complexions so well, curl their hair with such artfulness; they spend so much time adjusting themselves in front of their mirrors, that it would seem that there could only be a single gender in the entire town.

Women rather give themselves than offer themselves. Each day witnesses the consummation of the desires and hopes of each day. One only knows what it is to love and be loved. One busies himself only with that which they so falsely name, consummate pleasure.

Comme on remarque une rose au milieu des fleurs qui naissent dans l'herbe, on distingua Thémire de tant de belles. Elles n'eurent pas le temps d'être ses rivales: elles furent vaincues avant de la craindre. Dès qu'elle parut, Vénus ne regarda qu'elle. Elle appela les Grâces. Allez la couronner, leur dit-elle: de toutes les beautés que je vois, c'est la seule qui vous ressemble.

Chant Quatrième

Pendant que Thémire étoit occupée avec ses compagnes au culte de la déesse, j'entrai dans un bois solitaire: j'y trouvai le tendre Aristée. Nous nous étions vus le jour que nous allâmes consulter l'oracle; c'en fut assez pour nous engager à nous entretenir: car Vénus met dans le cœur, en la présence d'un habitant de Gnide, le charme secret que trouvent deux amis, lorsqu'après une longue absence ils sentent dans leurs bras le doux objet de leurs inquiétudes.

Ravis l'un de l'autre, nous sentîmes que notre cœur se donnoit; il sembloit que la tendre Amitié était descendue du ciel, pour se placer au milieu de nous. Nous nous racontâmes mille choses de notre vie. Voici, à peu près, ce que je lui dis:

Je suis né à Sybaris, où mon père Antiloque, était prêtre de Vénus. On ne met point, dans cette ville, de différence entre les voluptés & les besoins; on bannit tous les arts qui pourroient troubler un sommeil tranquille; on donne des prix, aux dépens du public, à ceux qui peuvent découvrir des voluptés nouvelles; les citoyens ne se souviennent que des bouffons qui les ont divertis, et ont perdu la mémoire des magistrats qui les ont gouvernés.

On y abuse de la fertilité du terroir, qui y produit une abondance éternelle; & les faveurs des dieux sur Sybaris ne servent qu'à encourager le luxe & la mollesse.

Les hommes sont si efféminés, leur parure est si semblable à celle des femmes; ils composent si bien leur teint; ils se frisent avec tant d'art; ils emploient tant de temps à se corriger à leur miroir, qu'il semble qu'il n'y ait qu'un sexe dans toute la ville.

Les femmes se livrent au lieu de se rendre: chaque jour voit finir les désirs et les espérances de chaque jour: on ne sait ce que c'est que d'aimer et d'être aimé; on n'est occupé que de ce qu'on appelle si faussement jouir.

Favors there exist only for themselves; and all those circumstances which so well accompany them, all those so highly prized little nothings, those contacts which always appear more grand, those little things which are worth so much—everything which anticipates a happy moment, many conquests instead of one, many consummations before the last—all of that is unknown at Sybaris.

Still, if women there had the least modesty, this feeble image of virtue would be able to give pleasure. But no, the eyes are used to seeing all, the ears to hearing all.

Far from receiving greater refinement from the multiplicity of pleasures, Sybarites are no longer able to distinguish one sentiment from another.

They spend their lives in a purely external joy. They leave off one pleasure which begins to displease them for another which will displease them anew. All that they imagine is but a new subject of disgust.

Their soul, incapable of sensing pleasure, seems only to possess refinement regarding pains. One citizen became wearied, all one night, of a rose which folded itself up in his bed.

Softness has so greatly weakened their bodies that they can't budge the least burden. They can hardly keep their own feet. The gentlest carriages make them faint. While, at their festivals, their stomachs fail them constantly.

They while away their lives on overturned sofas, without fatiguing themselves. When they go elsewhere to languish, they wear themselves out.

Unable to bear the weight of arms, timid before fellow-citizens, and cowardly before strangers, they are ready made slaves awaiting the first master.

From the moment I knew how to think, I was disgusted with the unhappy Sybarites. I love virtue, and I always fear the immortal gods. "No!" I said. "I will no longer breathe that poisonous air: all these slaves of softness are made to live in their fatherland and me to leave it."

I entered for the last time the temple, and, drawing near to the altar where my father had so often sacrificed, I cried out, "Great goddess, I abandon your temple and not your worship. On whatever spot of earth I may be, I will make incense burn for you. But it will be purer than that which they offer you here in Sybaris."

Les faveurs n'y ont que leur réalité propre; et toutes ces circonstances qui les accompagnent si bien, tous ces riens qui sont d'un si grand prix, ces engagements qui paraissent toujours plus grands, ces petites choses. qui valent tant, tout ce qui prépare un heureux moment, tant de conquêtes au lieu d'une, tant de jouissances avant la dernière: tout cela est inconnu à Sybaris.

Encore si elles avoient la moindre modestie, cette faible image de la vertu pourroit plaire: mais non; les yeux sont accoutumés à tout voir, & les oreilles à tout entendre.

Bien loin que la multiplicité des plaisirs donne aux Sybarites plus de délicatesse, ils ne peuvent plus distinguer un sentiment d'avec un sentiment.

Ils passent leur vie dans une joie purement extérieure: ils quittent un plaisir qui leur déplaît pour un plaisir qui leur déplaira encore; tout ce qu'ils imaginent est un nouveau sujet de dégoût.

Leur âme, incapable de sentir les plaisirs, semble n'avoir de délicatesse que pour les peines: un citoyen fut fatigué, toute une nuit, d'une rose qui s'étoit repliée dans son lit.

La mollesse a tellement affaibli leurs corps, qu'ils ne sçauroient remuer les moindres fardeaux; ils peuvent à peine se soutenir sur leurs pieds; les voitures les plus douces les font évanouir; lorsqu'ils sont dans les festins, l'estomac leur manque à tous les instants.

Ils passent leur vie sur des sièges renversés, sur lesquels ils sont obligés de se reposer tout le jour, sans être fatigués: ils sont brisés, quand ils vont languir ailleurs.

Incapables de porter le poids des armes, timides devant leurs concitoyens, lâches devant les étrangers, ils sont des esclaves tout prêts pour le premier maître.

Dès que je sçus penser, j'eus du dégoût pour la malheureuse Sybaris. J'aime la-vertu; et j'ai toujours craint les dieux immortels. Non, disois je, je ne respirerai pas plus longtemps cet air empoisonné: tous ces esclaves de la mollesse sont faits pour vivre dans leur patrie, et moi pour la quitter.

J'allai, pour la dernière fois, au temple; et, m'approchant des autels où mon père avait tant de fois sacrifié Grande Déesse, dis je à haute-voix, j'abandonne ton temple, et non pas ton culte; en quelque lieu de la terre que je sois, je ferai fumer pour toi de l'encens; mais il sera plus pur que celui qu'on t'offre à Sybaris.

I left and arrived in Crete. That isle is replete with the monuments of Cupid. One sees the bronzed bull, the work of Daedalus for betraying or for satisfying the distractions of Pasiphaessa; the labyrinth, the artifice of which Cupid alone knew how to escape; Phedre's tomb, which surprised the Sun as his mother had done; and the temple of Ariane, who, lost in deserts, abandoned by an ingrate, still did not repent of having followed him.

One sees the palace of Idomeneus there, whose return was no more happy than that of the other Greek captains. For those who escaped from the dangers of an angry natural element found their homes still more sinister. An angered Venus caused them to kiss perfidious wives, and they died by hands which they believed most dear.

I left that island, so odious to a goddess who ought some day to cause the happiness of my life.

I re-embarked and was carried by a tempest to Lesbos. That was still an isle little loved by Venus. She had taken modesty away from the countenances of the women, weakness from their bodies, and timidity from their souls. "Great Venus, let the Lesbian women burn from a legitimate fire; save human nature from horrors so many."

Mytilene is the capital of Lesbos. That is the home of the delicate Sappho. Immortal like the muses, that unfortunate girl burns with a fire which she can not extinguish. Odious to herself, finding her ennuies in her charms, she hates her gender and always pursues it. "How," she exclaimed, "can so empty a flame be so cruel? Cupid, you are a hundred times more fearful when you amuse yourself than when you are angered."

Finally I departed Lesbos, and fate led me to an island still more profane. That was Lemnos. Venus has no temple there. The Lemnians never pray to her. "We reject," they say, "a worship which softens the heart." The goddess has often punished them for it. But, without expiating their crime, they bear its penalty: always more impious to the degree they are more afflicted.

I regained the sea, always in search of some land dear to the gods. The winds bore me to Delos. For some months I stayed on that sacred isle. But, whether because the gods sometimes pre-empt us in that which comes to us, or whether because our soul retains from the divine, from which it derives, some weak knowledge of the future, I sensed that my destiny, my happiness even, called me into another country.

Je partis, et j'arrivai en Crète. Cette île est toute pleine de monuments de l'Amour. On y voit le taureau d'airain, ouvrage de Dédale, pour tromper ou satisfaire les égarements de Pasiphaé; le labyrinthe, dont l'Amour seul sut éluder l'artifice; le tombeau de Phèdre, qui étonna le Soleil, comme avait fait sa mère; et le temple d'Ariane, qui, désolée dans les déserts, abandonnée par un ingrat, ne se repentait pas encore de l'avoir suivi.

On y voit le palais d'Idoménée, dont le retour ne fut pas plus heureux que celui des autres capitaines grecs: car ceux qui échappèrent aux dangers d'un élément colère trouvèrent leur maison plus funeste encore. Vénus irritée leur fit embrasser des épouses perfides: et ils moururent de la main qu'ils croyoient la plus chère.

Je quittai cette île, si odieuse à une déesse qui devait faire quelque jour la félicité de ma vie.

Je me rembarquai; et la tempête me jeta à Lesbos. C'est encore une île peu chérie de Vénus: elle a ôté la pudeur du visage des femmes, la faiblesse de leur. corps, et la timidité de leur âme. Grande Vénus, laisse brûler les femmes de Lesbos d'un feu légitime; épargne à la nature humaine tant d'horreurs.

Mitylène est la capitale de Lesbos; c'est la patrie de la tendre Sapho. Immortelle comme les Muses, cette fille infortunée brûle d'un feu qu'elle ne peut éteindre. Odieuse à elle-même, trouvant ses ennuis dans ses charmes, elle hait son sexe, et le cherche toujours. Comment, dit-elle, une flamme si vaine peut-elle être si cruelle? Amour, tu es cent fois plus redoutable quand tu te joues, que quand tu t'irrites.

Enfin je quittai Lesbos; et le sort me fit trouver une île plus profane encore; c'était celle de Lemnos. Vénus n'y a point de temple: jamais les Lemniens ne lui adressèrent de vœux. Nous rejettons, disent-ils, un culte qui amollit les cœurs. La déesse les en a souvent punis: mais, sans expier leur crime, ils en portent la peine; toujours plus impies à mesure qu'ils sont plus affligés.

Je me remis en mer, cherchant toujours quelque terre chérie des dieux; les vents me portèrent à Délos. Je restai quelques mois dans cette île sacrée. Mais, soit que les dieux nous préviennent quelquefois sur ce qui nous arrive, soit que notre âme retienne de la divinité, dont elle est émanée, quelque faible connoissance de l'avenir, je sentis que mon destin, que mon bonheur même, m'appeloient dans un autre pays.

One night, as I was in that tranquil condition, in which the soul, holding more to itself, seems to be liberated from the chain which holds it subjected, there appeared to me, I knew not at first whether she were, mortal or goddess. An invisible charm overspread her. She was not beautiful like Venus, but she was enchanting like her. Her charms were not entirely regular, but taken altogether they enchanted. You would not find that which one admires there, but that which pricks. Her hair fell negligently about her shoulders, but that was a fortunate negligence. Her stature was charming. She had that air which nature only gives, and the secret of which nature hides even from painters. She beheld my astonishment and smiled upon it. Gods! What a smile! "I am," she said to me in a voice which drilled to my heart, "the second of the Graces. Venus, who sends me, wants to make you happy. But you must go to adore her in her temple at Cnidus." She flew off; my arms pursued her. My dream flew away with her. There was left for me only the sweet regret of no longer seeing her, mixed with the delight of having seen her.

Then I left the isle of Delos. I came to Cnidus. Immediately, I may say, I breathed love. I sensed—I can't very well express that which I felt. I did not yet love, but I expected to love. My heart warmed itself as if in the presence of some divine beauty. I went on and I saw, from afar, some young girls at play in the prairie. I was straightway carried toward them. "Silly me," I said. "I have all the distractions of love without being in love." My heart flew towards some unknown objects, and those objects disturbed it. I drew nearer. I saw lovely Themira. No doubt but we were made for each other. I beheld only her. And I believe that I should have died of sadness had she not cast some glances at me. "Great Venus," I cried, "since you owe to make me happy, ordain that it shall be with this shepherd-girl. I decline all the other lovelies. She alone can fulfill your promises and every prayer that I can ever make."

Fifth Chant

I continued to speak to young Aristeus of all my delicate loves. They made him sigh for his. I lifted his heart by begging him to relate them to me. Here is what he told me. I will forget nothing, for I am inspired by the same god who caused him to speak.

Une nuit que j'étais dans cet état tranquille où l'âme, plus à elle-même, semble être délivrée de la chaîne qui la tient assujettie; il m'apparut, je ne sçus pas d'abord si c'étoit une mortelle, ou une déesse. Un charme secret étoit répandu sur toute sa personne: elle n'étoit point belle comme Venus, mais elle étoit ravissante comme elle: tous ses traits n'étoient point réguliers, mais ils enchantoient tous ensemble: vous n'y trouviez point ce qu'on admire, mais ce qui pique: ses cheveux tomboient négligemment sur ses épaules, mais cette négligences étoit heureuse: sa taille étoit charmante; elle avoit cet air que la nature donne seule, & dont elle avoit cet air que la nature donne seule, & dont elle cache le secret aux peintres même. Elle vit mon étonnement; elle en sourit. Dieux! quel souris! Je suis, me dit-elle d'une voix qui pénétroit le cœur, la seconde des Grâces: Venus, qui m'envoie, veut te rendre heureux; mais il faut que tu ailles l'adorer dans son temple de Gnide. Elle fuit; mes bras la suivirent: mon songe s'envola avec elle; & il ne me resta qu'un doux regret de ne la plus voir, mêlé du plaisir de l'avoir vue.

Je quittai donc l'isle de Délos: j'arrivai a Gnide. Je puis dire que d'abord je respirai l'amour. Je sentis, je ne puis pas bien exprimer ce que je sentis. Je n'aimois pas encore, mais je cherchois a aimer; mon cœur s'échauffoit comme dans la présence de quelque beauté divine. J'avançai; & je vis, de loin, de jeunes filles qui jouoient dans la prairie: je fus d'abord entrainé vers elles. Insensé que je suis! disois-je, sans aimer, tous les égarement de l'amour: mon coeur vole déjà vers des objets inconnus; & ces objets lui donnent de l'inquiétude. J'approchai: je vis la charmante Thémire! Sans doute que nous étions faits l'un pour l'autre. Je ne regardai qu'elle; & je crois que je serais mort de douleur, si elle n'avait tourné sur moi quelques regards. Grande Vénus, m'écriai je, puisque vous devez me rendre heureux, faites que ce soit avec cette bergère! je renonce à toutes les autres beautés; elle seule peut remplir vos promesses & tous les vœux que je ferai jamais.

Chant Cinquième

Je parlois encore au jeune Aristée de mes tendres amours; ils lui firent soupirer les siens; je-soulageai son cœur, en le priant de me les raconter. Voici ce qu'il me dit; je n'oublierai rien; car je suis inspiré par le même dieu qui le faisoit parler.

"In all this narrative you will only find what is very simple. My adventures are only the sentiments of an affectionate heart, only my pleasures, only my pains. And just as my love for Camille makes the happiness of my life, so too it makes the entire story of my life.

"Camille is daughter to one of Cnidus' chief inhabitants. She is beautiful. She has an appearance which is going to engrave itself in every heart. Women with wishes to make beg the gods for the graces of Camille. Men who see her long to see her always or fear to see her again.

"She has a lovely stature, a noble but modest air, eyes lively and ready to be affectionate, characteristics made to go together, and charms invisibly arranged to tyrannise hearts.

"Camille makes no attempt to make herself up, but she is better made up than other women.

"She has a mind which nature almost uniformly refuses to beautiful women. She engages with equal readiness in things serious and gay. If you wish, she will reflect gravely. If you wish, she will make pleasantries like the Graces.

"The better mind one has, the more of it one will discover in Camille. There is about her something so naive, that she seems only to speak the language of the heart. Everything she says, everything she does has the charm of simplicity. You find always a naive shepherd-girl. Certain graces so light, so fine, so delicate make themselves noticed but are still better felt.

"With all of that Camille loves me. She is enchanted when she sees me, irritated when I leave her. And, as if I could live without her, she makes me promise to return. I tell her always that I love her. She believes me. I say that I adore her. She knows it. But she is delighted as if she hadn't known it. When I tell her that she makes the felicity of my life, she responds that I make the happiness of hers. In sum, she loves me so much that she could almost make me believe that I am worthy of her love.

"I saw Camille for a month without daring to tell her that I loved her and almost without daring to say it to myself. The more I found her lovable, the less I hoped to be he who could make her aware. 'Camille, your charms move me, but they tell me that I do not deserve you.'

"'I looked everywhere to forget you. I wanted to erase your lovely image from my mind. Oh! how happy I am! I could not succeed in that. That image remained in my mind and will live there forever.

Dans tout ce récit, vous ne trouverez rien que de très simple: mes aventures ne sont que les sentiments d'un cœur tendre, que mes plaisirs, que mes peines; &, comme mon amour pour Camille fait le bonheur, il fait aussi toute l'histoire de ma vie.

Camille est fille d'un des principaux habitants de Gnide; elle est belle; elle a une physionomie qui va se peindre dans tous les cœurs: les femmes qui font des souhaits demandent aux dieux les grâces de Camille; les hommes qui la voient veulent là voir toujours, ou craignent de la voir encore.

Elle, a une taille charmante, un air noble, mais modeste, des yeux vifs & tout prêts à être tendres; des traits faits exprès l'un pour l'autre, des charmes invisiblement assortis pour la tyrannie des cœurs.

Camille ne cherche point à se parer; mais elle est mieux parée que les autres femmes.

Elle a un esprit que la nature refuse presque toujours aux belles. Elle se prête également au sérieux & à l'enjouement. Si vous voulez, elle pensera sensément; si vous voulez, elle badinera comme les Grâces.

Plus on a d'esprit, plus on en trouve à Camille. Elle a quelque chose de si naïf, qu'il semble qu'elle ne parle que le langage du cœur. Tout ce qu'elle dit, tout ce qu'elle fait, a les charmes de la simplicité; vous trouvez toujours une bergère naïve. Des grâces si légères, si fines, si délicates, se font remarquer, mais se font encore mieux sentir.

Avec tout cela, Camille m'aime: elle est ravie quand elle me voit; elle est fâchée quand je la quitte; &, comme si je pouvois vivre sans elle, elle me fait promettre de revenir. Je lui dis toujours que je l'aime, elle me croit: je lui dis que je l'adore, elle le sait; mais elle est ravie, comme si elle ne le sçavoit pas. Quand je lui dis qu'elle fait la félicité de ma vie, elle me dit que je fais le bonheur de la sienne. Enfin, elle m'aime tant, qu'elle me ferait presque croire que je suis digne de son amour.

Il y avoit un mois que je voyois Camille, sans oser lui due que je l'aimois, & sans oser presque me le dire à moi-même: plus je la trouvais aimable, moins j'espérais d'être celui qui la rendrait sensible. Camille, tes charmes me touchoient; mais ils me disoient que je ne te méritois pas.

Je cherchois partout à t'oublier; je voulois effacer de mon cœur ton adorable image. Que je suis heureux! je n'ai pu y réussir; cette image y est restée, & elle y vivra toujours!

"I said to Camille: 'I loved the noise of the world, but I am pursuing solitude. I had some notions of ambition, but any longer I desire only your presence. I wanted to wander through distant climates, but any longer my heart is a citizen only of the places where you breathe. All that is not of you has vanished from before my eyes.

"Whenever Camille has spoken to me of her affection, she still has something to say to me. She believes that she has overlooked that which she has sworn to me a thousand times. I am so delighted to hear her that I sometimes feign not to believe her. There soon reigns between us that sweet silence which is the most delicate language of lovers.

"Whenever I've been away from Camille, I want to give her an account of whatever I've been able to see or hear. 'With what are you entertaining me?' she asks. 'Speak to me of our loves, or, if you have thought of nothing, if you have nothing to tell me, cruel one, let me speak.'

"Sometimes, in kissing me, she says to me, 'You are sad.' It is true, I tell her. But the sadness of lovers is delicious. I feel my tears flowing, and I don't know why, because you love me, and I have nothing to complain of, but I complain. Don't raise me from my languor. Allow me to sigh through my pains and pleasures all at once.

"In the emotions of love my soul is too stirred up. She is borne towards her happiness without to have consummated it, while presently I taste my sadness itself. Don't wipe away my tears. What can it matter that I cry, since I am happy?

"Sometimes Camille says to me: 'Do you love me?' Yes, I love you. 'But how do you love me?' Alas! I tell her, I love you as I loved you. For I can only compare the love I have for you to that which I have for you alone.

"I hear Camille praised by all who know her. Their praises move me as if they were personal to me. And I'm more flattered by them than [she] herself.

"When someone is with us, she 'speaks with so much spirit that I'm enchanted by her least sayings. But I would still more love that she said nothing.

"Whenever she shares friendship with someone, I could want to be he with whom she shares the friendship, except, all of a sudden, I reflect that then I would not be loved by her.

Je dis à Camille: J'aimois le bruit du monde, & je cherche la solitude; j'avois des vues d'ambition, & je ne désire plus que ta présence; je voulois errer sous des climats reculés, & mon cœur n'est plus citoyen que des lieux ou tu respires: tout ce qui n'est point toi s'est évanoui de devant mes yeux.

Quand Camille m'a parlé de sa tendresse, elle a encore quelque chose à me dire; elle croit avoir oublié ce qu'elle m'a juré mille fois. Je suis si charmé de l'entendre, que je feins quelquefois de ne la pas croire, pour qu'elle touche encore mon cœur: bientôt règne entre nous ce doux silence, qui est le plus tendre langage des amans.

Quand j'ai été absent de Camille, je veux lui rendre compte de ce que j'ai pu voir ou entendre. De quoi m'entretiens-tu? me dit-elle? parle-moi de nos amours: ou si tu n'as rien pensé, si tu n'as rien à me dire, cruel, laisse-moi parler.

Quelquefois elle me dit en m'embrassant: Tu es triste. Il est vrai, lui dis-je: mais la tristesse des amants est délicieuse; je sens couler mes larmes, et je ne sais pourquoi, car tu m'aimes; je n'ai point de sujet de me plaindre, & je me plains. Ne me retire point de la langueur où je suis; laisse-moi soupirer en même temps mes peines et mes plaisirs.

Dans-les transports de l'amour, mon âme est trop agitée; elle est entraînée vers son bonheur sans en jouir; au lieu qu'à présent je goûte ma tristesse même. N'essuie pont mes larmes: qu'importe que je pleure, puisque je suis heureux?

Quelquefois Camille me dit: Aime-moi. Oui, je t'aime. Mais comment m'aimes-tu? Hélas! lui dis-je, je t'aime comme je t'aimois: car je ne puis comparer l'amour que j'ai pour toi, qu'à celui que j'ai eu pour toi-même.

J'entends louer Camille par tous ceux qui la connoissent: ces louanges me touchent comme si elles m'étoient personnelles; & j'en suis plus flatté qu'elle-même.

Quand il y a quelqu'un avec nous, elle parle avec tant d'esprit, que je suis enchanté de ses moindres paroles; mais j'aimerais encore mieux qu'elle ne dît rien.

Quand elle fait des amitiés à quelqu'un, je voudrois être celui à qui elle fait des amitiés, quand, tout à coup, je fais réflexion que je ne serois point aimé d'elle.

"Be careful, Camille, of the impostor lovers! They will tell you that they love you, and they will speak truly. They will tell you that they love you as much as I, but, I swear, by the gods, I love you more.

"Whenever I perceive her from afar, I lose my mind. She draws near and my heart becomes agitated. I come up to her, and it seems that my soul wants to fly, that that soul belongs to Camille, and that she wants to become her soul.

"Sometimes I wish to acquire a favor of her. She refuses it to me, but, in an instant, grants me another. That is no ruse. Struggling with her modesty and her love, she wants both to deny me everything and to be able to grant me all.

"She says to me, 'does it not suffice that I love you? What can you long for besides my heart?' I want you, I told her, to commit for me a fault of love, and which great love justifies.

"Camille, if I should some day cease to love you, may the Fates[20] be betrayed and take that for the last of my days. May they wipe out the remainder of a life which I would find deplorable whenever I would recall the pleasures that I had had in loving!"

Aristeus sighed and stopped speaking. I saw well that he ceased speaking of Camille only to think of her.

Sixth Chant

While we spoke about our lives we lost our way, and, having wandered about for a long time, we came into a large prairie. Led by a path of flowers, we came to the foot of a hideous boulder. We saw a dark grotto; we went in, thinking it the residence of some mortal. My God! who could have thought that that place would be so fatal! I had hardly stepped my foot in when my whole body shook. My hair stood on end. An unseen hand bore me into that fatal inn. The more my heart shook, the more it sought to shake. "Friend," I cried out, "let us enter farther in; we might owe it to ourselves to increase our pains. I delved farther into that place where the sun shone never and the wind never rattled. I saw Jealousy there. Her face was more somber than frightful. She was surrounded by Paleness, Sadness, and Silence, and Boredoms [ennuies] flew around her. She blew on us, and placed our hands on her heart. She struck us on the head and we neither saw nor imagined anything but monsters. "Go yet farther in, unhappy mortals," she told us; "Go find a goddess more powerful than I."

Prends garde, Camille, aux impostures des amants. Ils te diront qu'ils t'aiment, & ils diront vrai: ils te diront qu'ils t'aiment autant que moi; mais je jure, par les dieux, que je t'aime davantage.

Quand je l'aperçois de loin, mon esprit s'égare: elle approche, & mon cœur s'agite: j'arrive auprès d'elle, & il semble que mon âme veut me quitter, que cette âme est à Camille, & qu'elle va l'animer.

Quelquefois je veux lui dérober une faveur; elle me la refuse, & dans un instant elle m'en accorde une autre. Ce n'est point un artifice: combattue par sa pudeur & son amour, elle voudroit me tout refuser, elle voudroit pouvoir me tout accorder.

Elle me dit: Ne vous suffit-il pas que je vous aime? que pouvez-vous désirer après mon cœur? Je désire, lui dis-je, que tu fasses pour moi une faute que l'amour fait faire & que le grand amour justifie.

Camille, si je cesse un jour de t'aimer, puisse la Parque se tromper, & prendre ce jour pour le dernier de mes jours! Puisse-t-elle effacer le reste d'une vie que je trouverois déplorable, quand je me souviendrois des plaisirs que j'ai eus en aimant!

Arístée soupira, & se tut; et je vis bien qu'il ne cessa de parler de Camille que pour penser à elle.

Chant Sixième

Pendant que nous parlions de nos amours, nous nous égarâmes, &, après avoir erré longtemps, nous entrâmes dans une grande prairie: nous fûmes conduits, par un chemin de fleurs, au pied d'un rocher affreux. Nous vîmes un antre obscur; nous y entrâmes, croyant que c'étoit la demeure de quelque mortel. O dieux! qui auroit pensé que ce lieu eût été si funeste? A peine y eus je mis le pied, que tout mon corps frémit, mes cheveux se dressèrent sur la tête. Une main invisible m'entraînoit dans ce fatal séjour: à mesure que mon cœur s'agitoit, il cherchoit à s'agiter encore. Ami, m'écriai-je, entrons plus avant, dussions-nous voir augmenter nos peines! J'avance dans ce lieu, où jamais le soleil n'entra, & que les vents n'agitèrent jamais. J'y vis la Jalousie; son aspect étoit plus sombre que terrible: la Pâleur, la Tristesse, le Silence l'entouroient, & les Ennuis voloient autour d'elle. Elle souffla sur nous, elle nous mit la main sur le cœur, elle nous frappa sur la tête; & nous ne vîmes, nous n'imaginâmes plus que des monstres. Entrez plus avant, nous dit-elle, malheureux mortels; allez trouver une déesse plus puissante que moi.

We saw a frightening divinity, lit up by the flaming tongues of serpents hissing about her head. That was Fury. She untied one of her serpents and tossed it on me. I wanted to take it, but straightway, without that I had felt a thing, it slid into my heart. I stood for a moment, dumbly. But from the moment its poison was spread through my veins, I imagined myself in the middle of infernos. My soul was inflamed and, in its violence, my entire body could scarce contain it. I was so agitated that it seemed to me that I squirmed beneath the whip of the Furies. We surrendered ourselves to our transports. We made the tour of that frightful grotto a hundred times. We went from Jealousy to Fury and from Fury to Jealousy, crying out, "Themira!" "Camille!" Had Themira or Camille come we would have torn them apart with our own hands.

Finally we found the light of day, which appeared to us demanding. We almost regretted having left the hideous grotto. We collapsed with fatigue, but even that rest seemed unbearable to us. Our eyes refused to yield our tears and our hearts were no longer able to create sighs.

Still I was tranquil for a moment. Sleep began to sprinkle her sweet poppies over me. Oh gods! Even my sleep became cruel. In it I saw images more terrible than the pale Shades. At every instant I awakened upon some infidelity of Themira's. I saw her . . . No! I do not yet dare to say it. That which I imagined only during the evening I found real in the horrors of that frightful sleep.

It will be necessary, then, I said to myself in getting up, that I avoid equally darkness and light. Themira! Cruel Themira agitates me like the Furies. Who had believed it, that my happiness would be to forget her forever!

Again I was gripped in furor. "Friend," I yelled out, "get up. Let's go exterminate that flock of sheep grazing in that prairie. Let's chase those shepherds whose loves are so peaceful." But no, I see a temple afar. It is perhaps that of Cupid. Let's go destroy it; let's go break his statue and make our furors fearful for him. We ran, and it seemed that the ardor to commit a crime gave us new strength. We crossed through woods, meadows, and plowed up fields. We weren't hindered, for even an instant. A hill bridled our path in vain. We climbed it. We entered the temple. It was consecrated to Bacchus. How great is the power of gods! Our fury was quickly abated. We beheld each other and noticed with some surprise the disarray we were in.

Nous vîmes une affreuse divinité, à la lueur des langues enflammées des serpents qui siffloient sur sa tète: c'étoit la Fureur. Elle détacha un de ses serpents, & le jeta sur moi: je voulus le prendre; déjà, sans que je l'eusse senti, il s'étoit glissé dans mon cœur. Je restai un moment comme stupide; mais, dès que le poison fut répandu dans mes veines, je crus être au milieu des enfers mon âme fut embrasée, &, dans sa violence, tout mon corps la contenoit à peine: j'étois si agité, qu'il me sembloit que je tournois sous le fouet des Furies. Nous nous abandonnâmes à nos transports; nous fîmes cent fois le tour de cet antre épouvantable nous allions de la Jalousie à la Fureur, & de la Fureur à la Jalousie nous criions, Thémire! nous criions, Camille! Si Thémire ou Camille étoient venues, nous les aurions déchirées de nos propres mains.

Enfin, nous trouvâmes la lumière du jour; elle nous parut importune, & nous regrettâmes presque l'antre affreux que nous avions quitté. Nous tombâmes de lassitude; & ce repos même nous parut insupportable. Nos yeux nous refusèrent des larmes, & notre cœur ne put plus former de soupirs.

Je fus pourtant un moment tranquille: le sommeil commençoit à verser sur moi ses doux pavots. O dieux! ce sommeil même devint cruel. J'y voyois des images plus terribles pour moi que les pâles Ombres: je me réveillois, à chaque instant, sur une infidélité de Thémire: je la voyois . . . Non, je n'ose encore le dire; & ce que j'imaginois seulement pendant la veille, je le trouvois réel dans les horreurs de cet affreux sommeil.

Il faudra donc, dis-je en me levant, que je fuie également les ténèbres & la lumière! Thémire, la cruelle Thémire, m'agite comme les Furies. Qui l'eût cru, que mon bonheur seroit de l'oublier pour jamais!

Un accès de fureur me reprit: Ami, m'écriai-je, lève-toi! Allons exterminer les troupeaux qui paissent dans cette prairie: poursuivons ces bergers dont les amours sont si paisibles. Mais non: je vois de loin un temple; c'est peut-être celui de l'Amour: allons le détruire, allons briser sa statue, & lui rendre nos fureurs redoutables. Nous courûmes; & il sembloit que l'ardeur de commettre un crime nous donnât des forces nouvelles: nous traversâmes les bois, les prés, les guérets; nous ne fûmes pas arrêtés un instant: une colline s'élevoit en vain, nous y montâmes; nous entrâmes dans le temple; il étoit consacré à Bacchus. Que la puissance des dieux est grande! Notre fureur fut aussitôt calmée. Nous nous regardâmes, & nous vîmes avec surprise le désordre où nous étions.

"Great god," I cried, "I thank you less for slacking my furor than for having saved me from a great crime." And, drawing near to the priestess, "we are beloved by the god whom you serve; he managed to quiet the transports by which we were agitated. We had hardly come into this place when we felt the presence of his favor. We wish to sacrifice to him. Deign to offer it on our behalf, divine priestess." I went to find a victim, and I brought it to her feet.

While the priestess readied the mortal blow, Aristeus recited the following sayings: "Divine Bacchus, you love to see joy upon the faces of men. Our pleasures are your worship, and you wish to be adored only by the happiest mortals.

"Sometimes you sweetly distract our reason; but when some cruel divinity has robbed us of it, you alone could be able to restore it.

"Black Jealousy holds Cupid in subjection; but you have deprived her of her sway over our hearts. You cause her to return to her own frightful domicile."

When the sacrifice was done, the whole people gathered about us. I related to the priestess how we had been tormented in Jealousy's domicile. Then, all at once, we heard a loud noise, a confused murmur of voices, and some musical instruments. We exited the temple and saw a troop of Bacchanalians draw nigh. They struck the ground with their thyrsuses, crying out "Euoi!" The old Silenus followed, seated on an ass. His head seemed to seek the ground and, whenever they let go his body, he balanced himself to compensate. The troop had faces stained with lees. Then followed Pan with his flute, and the Satyrs surrounded their king. Joy reigned amidst disorder. A lovable folly mixed together games, raillery, dances, and songs. At last I saw Bacchus. He was upon a chariot drawn by tigers, such as are seen at the Ganges at the limits of the universe, bearing joy and victory everywhere.

The beautiful Ariadne was at his side. Princess, you would still complain of Theseus' infidelity as the god takes your crown and mounts it in heaven. He wiped away your tears. Had you not ceased to cry, you would have made a god unhappier than yourself, who were a mere mortal. He said to you, "love me. Forget him and his perfidy. I make you immortal, that I may love you forever."

Grand Dieu! m'écriai-je, je te rends moins grâces d'avoir apaisé ma fureur, que de m'avoir épargné un grand crime. Et, m'approchant de la prêtresse: Nous sommes aimés du dieu que vous servez; il vient de calmer les transports dont nous étions agités; à peine sommes-nous entrés dans ce lieu, que nous avons senti sa faveur présente: nous voulons lui faire un sacrifice. Daignez l'offrir pour nous, divine prêtresse. J'allai chercher une victime, & je l'apportai à ses pieds.

Pendant que la prêtresse se préparait à donner le coup mortel, Aristée prononça ces paroles: Divin Bacchus, tu aimes à voir la joie sur le visage des hommes; nos plaisirs sont un culte pour toi; & tu ne veux être adoré que par les mortels les plus heureux.

Quelquefois tu égares doucement notre raison: mais, quand quelque divinité cruelle nous l'a ôtée, il n'y a que toi qui puisses nous la rendre.

La noire Jalousie tient l'Amour sous son esclavage; mais tu lui ôtes l'empire qu'elle prend sur nos cœurs; & tu la fais rentrer dans sa demeure affreuse.

Après que le sacrifice fut fait, tout le peuple s'assembla autour de nous; & je racontai à la prêtresse comment nous avions été tourmentés dans la demeure de la Jalousße. Et, tout à coup, nous entendîmes un grand bruit, et un mélange confus de voix & d'instruments de musique. Nous sortîmes du temple & nous vîmes arriver une troupe de bacchantes, qui frappaient la terre de leurs thyrses, criant à haute voix: Évhoé. Le vieux Silène suivait, monté sur son âne: sa tête sembloit chercher la terre; &, sitôt qu'on abandonnoit son corps, il se balançoit comme par mesure. La troupe avoit le visage barbouillé de lie. Pan paraissoit ensuite avec sa flûte, & les Satyres entouroient leur roi. La joie régnoit avec le désordre; une folie aimable mêloit ensemble les jeux, les railleries, les danses, les chansons. Enfin, je vis Bacchus: il étoit sur son char traîné par des tigres, tel que le Gange le vit au bout de l'univers, portant partout la joie et la victoire.

À ses côtés étoit la belle Ariane. Princesse, vous vous plaigniez encore de l'infidélité de Thésée, lorsque le dieu prit votre couronne, & la plaça dans le ciel. Il essuya vos larmes. Si vous n'aviez pas cessé de pleurer, vous aurez rendu un dieu plus malheureux que vous, qui n'étiez qu'une mortelle. Il vous dit: Aimez-moi; Thésée fuit; ne vous souvenez plus de son amour, oubliez jusqu'a sa perfidie. Je vous rends immortelle, pour vous aimer toujours.

I saw Bacchus step down from his chariot. I saw Ariadne step down. She went into the temple. She exclaimed, "lovable god, let us stay in this place and here sigh out our loves. Let us make this sweet climate benefit from eternal joy. Near these precincts the queen of hearts has set up her empire. Let the god of joy reign near her and increase the happiness of this already so fortunate people.

"As for me, great god, I already feel that I love you more. What! Could you some day seem to me still more lovable? Only the immortals may love to excess and still love further. They alone obtain more than they long for, and are more restrained when they long than in their consummations.

"You will be my perpetual love here. In heaven one busies himself only with glory. Only on earth, and in bucolic fields, does one know how to love. And while this troop abandons itself to frenetic joy, my joy, my sighs, and even my tears will tell you ceaselessly of my love."

The god smiled at Ariadne. He led her into the holy of holies. Our hearts were overcome with joy. We felt a divine emotion. Caught up in the distractions of Silenus and the transports of the Bacchanalians, we grabbed a thyrsus and melted into the dances and concerts.

Seventh Chant

We departed Bacchus's sacred precincts. But soon we thought that we felt our ills had only been postponed. True, we did not have that furor which had agitated us. But somber Sadness had seized upon our souls and we were consumed by suspicions and worries.

It seemed to us that the cruel goddesses had agitated us only to make us confront the evils for which we were destined.

At times we longed for the temple of Bacchus. Soon we were borne towards that of Cnidus. We wished to see Themira and Camille, those powerful objects of our love and jealousy.

But we had none of those sweet reflections which one is wont to feel when, about to see again that which he loves, the soul is already ecstatic and seems to taste in anticipation the happiness she expects [in the event].

"Perhaps," said Aristeus, "I will discover Lucas, the shephered, with Camille. How do I know that he isn't speaking to her right now? O! gods! the faithless one enjoys listening to him."

Je vis Bacchus descendre de son char; je vis descendre Ariane; elle entra dans le temple. Aimable Dieu, s'écria-t-elle, restons dans ces lieux, & soupirons-y nos amours. Faisons jouir ce doux climat d'une joie éternelle. C'est auprès de ces lieux que la reine des cœurs a posé son empire; que le dieu de la joie règne auprès d'elle, & augmente le bonheur de ces peuples déjà si fortunés.

Pour moi, grand Dieu, je sens déjà que je t'aime davantage. Quoi! tu pourrais quelque jour me paraître encore plus aimable! Il n'y a que les immortels qui puissent aimer à l'excès, & aimer toujours davantage; il n'y a qu'eux qui obtiennent plus qu'ils n'espèrent, & qui sont plus bornés quand ils désirent que quand ils jouissent.

Tu seras ici mes éternels amours. Dans le ciel, on n'est occupé que de sa gloire; ce n'est que sur la terre & dans les lieux champêtres, que l'on sçait aimer. Et pendant que cette troupe se livrera à une joie insensée, ma joie, mes soupirs et mes larmes même, te rediront sans cesse mes amours.

Le dieu sourit à Ariane; il la mena dans le sanctuaire. La joie s'empara de nos cœurs: nous sentîmes une émotion divine. Saisis des égarements de Silène & des transports des bacchantes, nous prîmes un thyrse, & nous nous mêlâmes dans les danses & dans les concerts.

Chant Septième

Nous quittâmes les lieux consacrés à Bacchus; mais bientôt nous crûmes sentir que nos maux n'avoient été que suspendus. Il est vrai que nous n'avions point cette fureur qui nous avait agités; mais la sombre tristesse avoit saisi notre âme, & nous étions dévorés de soupçons & d'inquiétudes.

Il nous sembloit que les cruelles déesses ne nous avoient agités que pour nous faire pressentir des malheurs auxquels nous étions destinés.

Quelquefois nous regrettions le temple de Bacchus; bientôt nous étions entraînés vers celui de Gnide: nous voulions voir Thémire et Camille, ces objets puissants de notre amour & de notre jalousie.

Mais nous n'avions aucune de ces douceurs que l'on a coutume de sentir, lorsque, sur le point de revoir ce qu'on aime, l'âme est déjà ravie, et semble goûter d'avance tout le bonheur qu'elle se promet.

Peut-être, dit Aristée, que je trouverai le berger Lycas avec Camille; que sçais je s'il ne lui parle pas dans ce moment? O dieux! l'infidèle prend plaisir à l'entendre!

"The other day folk were saying," I responded, "that Thyrsites, who so much loved Themira, was due to come to Cnidus. He loved her, and doubtlessly he loves her still. It will be necessary for me to compete for a heart which I thought already mine."

"Lucas sang my Camille's praises the other day. How incensed I was, while I was delighted to hear her praised."

"I remember how Thyrsites brought new flowers to my Themira. Miserable creature that I am, she placed them on her breast!" 'This is a present from Thyrsites,' she said. Ah! I ought to have snatched them up and crushed them beneath my feet."

"Not long ago I went with Camille to offer a sacrifice of two turtle doves to Venus. They escaped me and flew off into the skies."

"I had written my name with that of Themira on some trees. I wrote down my love, and read and re-read it endlessly. One morning I discovered they had been erased."

"Camille, don't destroy the hopes of an unhappy soul who loves you. The love that one frustrates can have all the effects of hate."

"The first Cnidian who looks upon my Themira, I will chase right up to the temple and I will punish him even were he at Venus' feet."

Meanwhile, we reached the sacred grotto from which the goddess pronounces her oracles. The people were like the waves of a troublous sea. While some came to listen, others went to look for their answers.

We joined the crowd. I lost the happy Aristeus, who had already embraced his Camille. As for me, I was still seeking my Themira.

Finally, I found her. I felt my jealousy increase two-fold at the sight of her. I felt my first furors begin anew. But she looked at me, and I became still. Thus do the gods chase the Furies, whenever they stray outside their infernos.

"My god," she told me, "how you have cost me some tears! I feared to have lost you forever." That speech made me tremble. "I went to consult the oracle. I did not ask whether you loved me, alas! I only wanted to know whether you yet lived. Venus responded that you would love me forever."

"Forgive an unfortunate soul who could have hated you, if his soul were capable of it," I said to her. "The gods, in whose hands I am, can deprive me of reason. Those gods, Themira, can not rob me of my love.

On disoit l'autre jour, repris je, que Tirsis, qui a tant aimé Thémire, dévoit arriver à Gnide; il l'a aimée, sans doute qu'il l'aime encore: il faudra que je dispute un cœur que je croyois tout à moi.

L'autre jour, Licas chantoit ma Camille: que j'étois insensé! j'étois ravi de l'entendre louer.

Je me souviens que Tßrsis porta à ma Thémire des fleurs nouvelles. Malheureux que je suis! elle les a mises sur son sein! C'est un présent de Tirsis, disoit-elle. Ah! j'aurois dû les arracher, & les fouler à mes pieds.

Il n'y a pas longtemps que j'allois, avec Camille, faire à Vénus un sacrifice de deux tourterelles; elles m'échappèrent, & s'envolèrent dans les airs.

J'avois écrit sur des arbres mon nom avec celui de Thémire; j'avois écrit mes amours je les lisois et les relisois sans cesse: un matin, je les trouvai effacées.

Camille, ne désespère point un malheureux qui t'aime: l'amour, qu'on irrite, peut avoir tous les effets de la haine.

Le premier Gnidien qui regardera ma Thémire, je le poursuivrai jusque dans le temple; & je le punirai, fût-il aux pieds de Vénus.

Cependant nous arrivâmes près de l'antre sacré où la déesse rend ses oracles. Le peuple était comme les flots de la mer agitée: ceux-ci venaient d'entendre, les autres allaient chercher leur réponse.

Nous entrâmes dans la foule; je perdis l'heureux Aristée déjà il avoit embrassé sa Camille; & moi je cherchois encore ma Thémire.

Je la trouvai enfin. Je sentis ma jalousie redoubler à sa vue, je sentis renaître mes premières fureurs. Mais elle me regarda; & je devins tranquille. C'est ainsi que les dieux renvoient les Furies, lorsqu'elles sortent des enfers.

O dieux! me dit-elle, que tu m'as coûté de larmes! Trois fois le soleil a parcouru sa carrière; je craignois de t'avoir perdu pour jamais: cette parole me fait trembler. J'ai été consulter l'oracle. Je n'ai point demandé si tu m'aimais; hélas! je ne voulois que savoir si tu vivois encore. Vénus vient de me répondre que tu m'aimes toujours.

Excuse, lui dis-je, un infortuné qui t'aurait haïe, si son âme en était capable. Les dieux, dans les mains desquels je suis, peuvent me faire perdre la raison: ces dieux, Thémire, ne peuvent pas m'ôter mon amour.

"Cruel Jealousy stirred me up, just as they torture criminal shades in Tartarus. I derive this advantage from it, that I better feel the happiness which it is to be loved by you, after the frightful encounter in which I was faced with the fear of losing you.

"Come with me now; come into this secluded woods. By force of love I must expiate the crimes which I have committed. It is a great crime, Themira, to believe you unfaithful."

Never were Elysian woods, which the gods made expressly for the tranquility of the Shades which they cherished; never were Dodonian forests, which speak to humans about their future happiness; nor Hesperidean gardens, in which trees are bowed by the weight of the gold of which their fruit is made—none were more charming than this forest enchanted by Themira's presence.

I recall that a Satyr, who chased a fleeing, tearful nymph, saw us and stopped. "Happy lovers," he yelled. "Your eyes know how to hear and respond to one another. Your sighs are repaid with sighs. But me, I spend my life on the trail of a ferocious shepherdess, unhappy while I pursue her, unhappier still when I catch her."

A young nymph, alone in the woods, noticed us and sighed. "No," said she, "it is only to heighten my torment that cruel Cupid causes me to witness so affectionate a lover."

We found Apollo seated by a fountain. He had followed Diana, whom a shy stag had led into this forest. I recognized her by her blond hair and the immortal herd by which she's always surrounded. He tuned his lyre; she attracted the rocks. The trees followed her; the lions remained motionless. But we went more deeply into the forests, vainly summoned by that divine harmony.

And where do you think I found Cupid? He was on Themira's lips. Next I found him on her breasts. He escaped to her feet, and I found him there too. He hid behind her knees. I followed him. I would always have found him if Themira, all in tears, Themira frustrated, had not stopped me. He had reached his last hide-away. She is so lovely that he knows not how to leave her. Just so does the delicate warbler, chained by fright and love to her little ones, remain motionless beneath the greedy hand that draws near, and is unable to surrender them.

La cruelle Jalousie m'a agité, comme dans le Tartare on tourmente les ombres criminelles. J'en tire cet avantage, que je sens mieux le bonheur qu'il y a d'être aimé de toi, après l'affreuse situation où m'a mis la crainte de te perdre.

Viens donc avec moi, viens dans ce bois solitaire: il faut qu'à force d'aimer j'expie les crimes que j'ai faits. C'est un grand crime, Thémire, de te croire infidèle.

Jamais les bois de l'Élysée, que les-dieux ont faits exprès pour la tranquillité des ombres qu'ils chérissent; jamais les forêts de Dodone, qui parlent aux humains de leur félicité future; ni les jardins des Hespérides, dont les arbres se courbent sous le poids de l'or qui compose leurs fruits, ne furent plus charmants que ce bocage enchanté par la présence de Thémire.

Je me souviens qu'un satyre, qui suivoit une nymphe qui fuyoit toute éplorée, nous vit, & s'arrêta. Heureux amants! s'écria-t-il, vos yeux sçavent s'entendre et se répondre; vos soupirs sont payés par des soupirs! Mais moi, je passe ma vie sur les traces d'une bergère farouche; malheureux pendant que je la poursuis, plus malheureux encore lorsque je l'ai atteinte.

Une jeune nymphe, seule dans ce bois, nous aperçut et soupira. Non, dit-elle, ce n'est que pour augmenter mes tourments, que le cruel Amour me fait voir un amant si tendre.

Nous trouvâmes Apollon assis auprès d'une fontaine. Il avoit suivi Diane, qu'un daim timide avoit menée dans ces bois. Je le reconnus à ses blonds cheveux, et à la troupe immortelle qui étoit autour de lui. Il accordoit sa lyre; elle attire les rochers; les arbres la suivent, les lions restent immobiles. Mais nous entrâmes plus avant dans les forêts, appelés en vain par cette divine harmonie.

Où croyez-vous que je trouvai l'Amour? Je le trouvai sur les lèvres de Thémire; je le trouvai ensuite sur son sein; il s'était sauvé à ses pieds: je l'y trouvai encore; il se cacha sous ses genoux: je le suivis; et je l'aurais toujours suivi, si Thémire tout en pleurs, Thémire irritée, ne m'eût arrêté. Il était à sa dernière retraite: elle est si charmante qu'il ne sauroit la quitter. C'est ainsi qu'une tendre fauvette, que la crainte et l'amour, retiennent sur ses petits, reste immobile sous la main avide qui s'approche, & ne peut consentir à les abandonner.

Unhappy me! Themira listened to my urgings, and she was not softened. She heard my prayers, and she became more severe. Finally, I was bold. She became indignant; I trembled. She seemed angry, and I cried. She pushed me away, and I fell. I felt that my sighs were going to be my last sighs, had not Themira placed a hand on my heart and resuscitated me.

"No," said she, "I am not so cruel as you. For I have never wished to make you die, while you wish to bear me into the night of the tomb.

"Open your dying eyes unless you wish that mine should close forever."

She kissed me. I received grace, alas, without hope of becoming guilty.

End of *The Temple de Gnide*

[Since the following piece seems to me to be by the same author, I've thought it necessary to translate it and place it here.]

One day as I wandered about the woods of Idalia I found Cupid asleep, hidden beneath some flowers and covered with some myrtle branches which swayed gently in the breaths of zephyrs. The Games and Laughters who always follow him had gone to make folly far from him. He was alone. I had Cupid in my power. His bow and his quiver were at his side, and, had I wanted, I could have stolen the weapons of Cupid. Cephise took the bow of the greatest of the gods. She put an arrow in it, without my having noticed, and fired it at me. I said to her, smiling, take a second one; wound me again. That one was too gentle. She wanted to line up another arrow; it fell on her foot, and she cried sweetly. "That was the heaviest arrow in Cupid's quiver!" She picked it up again and made it fly. It struck me, and I fell. Ah! Cephise, you wish to kill me, then? She drew near to Cupid. "He sleeps deeply," she said, "he is worn out from shooting his arrows. One must pick some flowers in order to bind his feet and hands." Ah! I can't agree to that, because he has always favored us. "Then I will take his weapons," she said, "and shoot him with an arrow with all my strength." But he will awaken, I told her. "Very well! Let him wake up. What will he be able to do besides wound us still further?" No! no; let him sleep. We will remain near him and thereby will be all the more aroused.

Malheureux que je suis! Thémire écouta mes plaintes, et elle n'en fut point attendrie: elle entendit mes prières, et elle devint plus sévère. Enfin, je fus téméraire; elle s'indigna: je tremblai; elle me parut fâchée: je pleurai; elle me rebuta: je tombai; et je sentis que mes soupirs alloient être mes derniers soupirs, si Thémire n'avoit mis la main sur mon cœur, et n'y eût ramené la vie.

Non, dit-elle, je ne suis pas si cruelle que toi; car je n'ai jamais voulu te faire mourir, et tu veux m'entraîner dans la nuit du tombeau.

Ouvre ces yeux mourans, si tu ne veux que les miens se⁻ fermént pour jamais.

Elle m'embrassa: je reçus ma grâce, hélas! sans espérance de devenir coupable.

Fin du *Temple de Gnide*

[Comme la pièce suivante m'a paru être du même auteur, j'ai cru devoir la traduire & la mettre ici.]

Un jour que j'errois dans les bois d'Idalie avec la jeune Céphise, je trouvai l'Amour qui dormoit caché sur des fleurs, & couvert par quelques branches de myrthe qui cédoient docement aux haleines des Zéphirs, Les Jeux and les Ris, qui le suivent toujours, étoient allé folâtrer loin de lui: il étoit seul. J'avois l'Amour en mon pouvoir; son arc & son carquois étoient a ses côtés; & si j'avois voulu, j'aurois volé les armes de l'Amour. Céphise prit l'arc du plus grand des dieux: elle y mit un trait, sans que je m'en apperçusse, & le lança contre moi. Je lui dis en souriant: Prends-en un second; fais-moi une autre blessure; celle-ci est trop douce. Elle voulut ajuster un autre trait; il lui tomba sur le pied; & elle cria docement: C'étoit le trait le plus pesant qui fut dans le carquois de l'Amour! Elle le reprit, le fit voler; il me frappa, je me baissai: Ah! Céphise, tu veux donc me faire mourir? Elle s'aprocha de l'Amour. Il dort profondément, dit-elle; il s'est fatigué à lancer ses traits. Il faut cueillir des fleurs, pour lui lier les pieds & les mains. Ah! je n'y puis consentir; car il nous a toujours favorisés. Je vais donc, dit-elle, prendre ses armes, & lui tirer une flèche de toute ma force. Mais il se réveillera, lui dis-je. Eh bien! qu'il se réveille: que pourra-t-il faire que nous blesser davantage? Non, non; laissons-le dormir; nous resterons auprès de lui; & nous en serons plus enflammés.

Then Cephise picked some myrtle leaves and roses. She said, "I want to cover Cupid. The Games and Laughters will look for him but will no longer be able to find him." She threw them over him and laughed to see the small god nearly buried. "But what do I find so funny?" she said. "It's necessary to clip his wings so that there should no longer be fickle men on earth. For this god goes from heart to heart bearing inconstancy everywhere." She took the scissors, sat down, and, taking into her hands the ends of Cupid's golden wings—I felt my heart seized with fear. "Stop, Cephise." She didn't listen to me. She clipped the peaks of Cupid's wings, dropped the scissors, and fled.

When he awakened he wanted to fly. He sensed a weight that he did not know. He saw on the flowers the tips of his wings. He began to cry. Jupiter, who noticed him from on high in Olympus, sent a cloud to him to carry him into the palace of Cnidus and lay him upon Venus' breast. "Mother," he said, "I beat my wings upon your breast. Someone has clipped my wings. What will become of me?" "My son," the beautiful Cyprus said, "don't cry. Stay on my breast and do not stir. The warmth will cause them to grow again. Don't you see that they are longer? Kiss me; they are growing. You will soon have them just as you did. I see already their peaks arraying themselves. Just a moment . . . that's enough. Fly, fly, my son." "Yes," he said, "I'm going to risk it." He flew. He landed near Venus and returned at once to her breast. He made another start and landed a little farther off. Again he came to Venus' breast. He kissed her and she smiled at him. He kissed her again and chatted amiably with her. Finally he rose into the skies, from which he reigns over all nature.

Cupid, in order to revenge himself on Cephise, made her the most fickle of beautiful women. He caused her to burn with a new desire each day. She has loved me. She has loved Daphnis. And now she is loving Cleon. Cruel Eros, it is I that you are punishing. I want to bear the penalty of her crime, but have you not some other torment to make me suffer?

End

Céphise prit alors des feuilles de myrthe & des roses. Je veux, dit-elle, en couvrir l'Amour. Les Jeux & les Ris le chercheront, & ne pourront plus le trouver. Elle les jetta sur lui; & elle rioit de voir le petit dieu presqu'enséveli. Mais à quoi m'amusai-je, dit-elle? Il faut lui couper les aîles, afin qu'il n'y ait plus sur la terre d'hommes volages; car ce dieu va de coeur en cœur,& porte par-tout l'inconstance. Elle prit ses ciseaux, s'assit; &, tenant d'une main le bout des aîles dorées de l'Amour, je sentis mon cœur frappé de crainte. Arrête, Céphise. Elle n'm'entendit pas. Elle coupa le sommet des aîles de l'Amour, laissa ses ciseaux, & s'enfuit.

Lorsqu'il se fut réveillé, il voulut voler; & il sentit un poids qu'il ne connoissoit pas. Il vit sur les fleurs le bout de ses aîles; il se mit à pleurer. Jupiter, qui l'aperçut du haut de l'Olympe, lui envoya un nuage qui le porta dans le palais de Gnide, & le posa sur le sein de Vénus. Ma Mère, dit-il, je battois de mes aîles sur votre sein; on me les a coupées: que vais-je devenir? Mon fils, dit la belle Chypris, ne pleurez point; restez sur mon sein, ne bougez pas; la chaleur va les faire renaître. Ne voyez-vous pas qu'elles sont plus grandes? Embrassez-moi: elles croissent: vous les aurez bientôt comme vous les aviez; j'en vois déjà le sommet qui se dore: dans un moment . . . C'est assez: volez, volez, mon fils. Oui, dit-il, je vais me hasarder. Il s'envola; il se reposa auprès de Vénus, & revint d'abord sur son sein. Il reprit l'essor; il alla se reposer un peu plus loin, & revint encore sur le sein de Vénus. Il l'embrassa; elle lui sourit: il l'embrassa encore, & badina avec elle; & enfin il s'éleva dans les airs, d'où il règne sur toute la nature.

L'Amour, pour se venger de Céphise, l'a rendue la plus volage de toutes les belles. Il la fait bruler chaque jour d'une nouvelle flamme. Elle m'a aimé; elle a aimé Daphnis; & elle aime aujourd'hui Cléon. Cruel Amour, c'est moi que vous punissez! Je veux bien porter la peine de son crime: mais n'auriez vous point d'autres tourmens a me faire souffrir?

Fin

Commentary

Commentary on *Le Temple de Gnide,* must begin by noting that the fable conveys Montesquieu's conception of man's duties. Though hated by Rousseau for its seductive lying in behalf of the cause of truth, the fable speaks to our immediate concern. Montesquieu thought it of some value, Rousseau notwithstanding. He was still making corrections to its "preface"—the seat of the lie—virtually on the eve of his death. The fable teaches that law as a guide for individuals is preferable to reason. It describes poetically the transition from the ancient sway of Helen and Achilles to the worship of law-abiding men and women. The condition or requirement for this transition is that reason—what is best in man—be content to leave the prize for beauty to what is lawful.

Our heroines and heroes in this voluptuous narrative are named Themira and Camille, the loveliest maidens at Cnidus, and their suitors, Aristeus and our unnamed narrator whom, for good reason, I will call Everyman. Venus rules in Cnidus. And she regularly rewards the most beautiful woman on earth, after women compete for her regards. Aristeus loves Camille, that namesake of Saturn's daughter who threatened to conquer Aeneas and his band. Everyman loves Themira, namesake of Themis, goddess of law and order, justice personified, established law and custom.

Women competed before Venus for the prize Helen so often won. How lucky, then, Everyman, when Venus awards the prize of beauty to Themira, "of all the beautiful women *I see!*" Aristeus wins the hand of Camille, defeating his arch rival, Lucas, Zeus' namesake. Everyman's rival is Thersites, namesake to that vulgar democrat who stirred Odysseus' ire. Everyman wins the hand of the New Helen. Themira, the New Helen, is to modernity as Helen is to Achaia and Troy. Camille would not condescend to compete. Venus did not see her! Everyman was born in Sybaris. Nevertheless, he was able to be inspired by the same god that inspired Aristeus, namesake of the best of men. Everyman and Aristeus were friends—perhaps because Aristeus' love, choosing not to compete for the prize of beauty, makes it unnecessary for Everyman and Aristeus to compete. To tell the truth, however, Everyman's love seemed to him worthy the prize independent of Venus's judgment. He could see no one else.

This sensuous fable is easy to understand, and worthy, Rousseau notwithstanding. By portraying the emergence of law-abidingness into its rightful place of honor, it eliminates the need to apologize for human conventions. Thereby it contributes to illuminate the central paradox in Montesquieu's philosophy. He stands out in the long line of modern political philosophers from Locke to Kant as the one who does not found a view of society's origins upon the idea of a social contract or anything like a social contract. Not only would such a view be inconsistent with the correct understanding of a constitution, the sway of a particular ignorance, but, figuratively, it would substitute the judgment about what is worthy of the various multitude of men (supposing any real chance of untutored agreement) for the superior judgment of Venus.

Another way to state the figurative conclusion is to say that Montesquieu avoids the peril implied in the social contract, of founding every human society on nothing more substantial than the whims and caprices of men. Every contract must be referred to its makers for its authoritative sense. Each maker is always authoritative as to what he intended. The variety of human opinions about the good suggests differing opinions about the aim of a contract—a diversity which cannot be overcome by *post facto* philosophic speculations. The device of the fable, *Le Temple de Gnide,* opens this inquiry to view in a way that, perhaps, no other device can do.

Notes

1. David Hume, *Essays Moral and Political* (London: Longmans, Green, and Co., 1889), vol. 1, 54, to Gilbert Elliott.

2. ibid.

3. Roger B. Oake, "Montesquieu and Hume," *Modern* Language *Quarterly,* vol. 2, March & June, 1941.

4. *Memorabilia,* XIII, iv, 1. He did not, however, concede that he got the idea of Socrates's ill health from Xenophon, whom he called one of "the greatest geniuses."

5. Plato, *Apology,* translated by Thomas G. West and Grace S. West (Ithaca, NY: Cornell Univ. Press, 1984), 26.

6. Memorabilia, IV, ii, 33.

7. Plato, *Republic,* 522d.

8. Cf., the Complaints of Ajax, in Ovid, *Metamorphoses, XIII, 56.*

9. Plato, *Apology.*

10. Cf., Hume's expectations for himself in his "Autobiography."

11. Op. cit.

12. One might compare Pericles' "funeral oration" in Thucydides with Montesquieu's portrait of French manners in *Esprit des Lois,* XIX to see how complete the comparison may be between Athens and France. Then see *Temple de Gnide,* where Montesquieu does not name but describes Athens in terms borrowed from Pericles, Third Chant, para. 13.

13. "Essai touchant les loix naturelles et la distinction du juste et de l'injuste."

14. Jean Jacques Rousseau, *Les reveries d'un promeneur solitaire* (Paris: Garnier-Flammarion, 1964), 77.

15. ibid., 81: ". . . it's necessary to subtract from the educated public the multitudes of vulgar and credulous readers upon whom the manuscript's history, recounted by a serious author with an air of good faith, has really imposed itself, and who have drunk fearlessly from an ancient chalice the very poison they would at least have suspected had it been presented to them in a modern carafe."

16. De la Fontaine, *Fables* (Paris: Bordas, 1964), "Dedicace," 35.

17. ibid., "Préface," 39. "two points; useful and pleasant inventions: those are the things that have introduced sciences among men. Aesop discovered a singular art for connecting the one with the other." "And since by defining the point, the line, the surface, and by other very familiar principles, we arrive at certain understandings that ultimately measure the heavens and earth, so, too, by the reasonings and consequences that folk can deduce from these fables, they shape their judgment and their morals, they make themselves capable of great things."

18. Tasso, Torquato, *Jérusalem délivrée*, trans. By J.-B. de Mirabaud, 1724.

19. On the island of Cyprus, Cnidus is in Asia Minor.

20. The three goddesses, Clotho, Lachésis, Atropos. They appear in Book X of Plato's *Republic* similarly.

Chapter 2

Montesquieu's *Lysimachus*

Translation and Commentary[1]

Preface

There is no extant record of an English translation of the last work of Montesquieu published in his lifetime. Scholars have traditionally considered the *Lysimaque* of little significance (with the apparent exception of C. Rosso, whose work is discussed below). The brief moral fable has been deemed by the authoritative biographer of Montesquieu, "no more than an elegant essay by a courtier."[2] David Lowenthal, in his comprehensive account of Montesquieu's relationship to the classics, argues that a philosophical morality is developed in none of Montesquieu's works.[3] Since the *Lysimaque* presents an account of the character and form of the relationship between a philosopher and, on the one hand, a tyrant and, on the other hand, an enlightened monarch, it is necessary to conclude that Lowenthal accepts or agrees with Shackleton's account of that dialogue.[4] In this view, the *Lysimaque* would not properly constitute a source of reflections on counsel in the tradition of Machiavelli or Sir Thomas More. But insofar as that leaves us no such source in Montesquieu's writings we encounter the difficulty of defending the judgment that Montesquieu's developed philosophy is amoral if not immoral.

In general, Leo Strauss has demonstrated that the charge of amorality is the traditional attack on philosophy. And for that reason alone, if none other, the practice of a philosophic politics has been incumbent upon philosophers. In raising the question of Montesquieu's morality, we necessarily encounter the question of his philosophic politics. "In what then does philosophic politics consist? In satisfying the city that the philosophers are not atheists, that they do not desecrate everything sacred to the city, that they reverence what the city reverences, that they are not subversives, in short, that they are not irresponsible adventurers but good citizens and even the best citizens."[5] To be certain: it is the end of philosophic politics to render it impossible for one ordinarily to arrive at the judgment that the philosophers' philosophy is amoral if not immoral.

We must reconsider Montesquieu because the traditional scholarly opinion of Montesquieu requires one of two equally interesting but unstated conclusions: either Montesquieu failed in his practice of philosophic politics or the circumstances in which he labored had radically altered the conditions of philosophy.

Introduction

A particular reason for reconsidering the question of morality in Montesquieu stems from recent American contributions to Montesquieu scholarship. It is now clear that the American polity owes a far greater debt to Montesquieu than that derived from the idea of a separation of powers.[6] It is now seriously suggested that the American regime is more fundamentally Montesquieuian than Lockeian.[7] And it is being debated whether the principles of modern liberalism as especially manifested in the American regime do not derive rather from the Founding Fathers' appreciation of Montesquieu's radical correction of modernity's initial impulses.[8] Hence, we confront the necessity of demonstrating how an amoral philosophy (science) can be the source of a specific morality (regime). This is not intended in terms of the contemporary discourse *vis-à-vis* Skinner's rational community. It rather confronts the difficulty Rousseau addressed in his criticism of modernity's attempt to democratize philosophy. That endeavor, he held, ends by destroying the basis of philosophy, by reducing science to technology.

From that perspective, modern political philosophy is still closer to the ancient tradition than it is close to contemporary science. At its origins, modern philosophy still confronted the fundamental question: whether the sphere of morality is closed or open to the sphere of philosophy. A philosophical morality, so far as there is such, would be the ground upon which the philosopher experiences the necessity that he concern himself with the sphere of morality not as a seeker of truth but as a good man. The legislating philosopher who neither experiences nor imagines any such necessity would constitute a moral wonder. And the chief wonder for good men at least would be that they should have the patience to hear him.

It is perhaps a less courageous path to challenge the established view that Montesquieu developed no philosophical morality than to wonder at his handiwork. But, if precedence may serve, it is the same path that Rosso follows, though to a different end. His skillfully written *Montesquieu Moralista*[9] reduces the problem of the morality of the philosopher to the question of human morality itself. That is, whoever inquires into the facts of human morality, in order to state what is among men, is in that act a moral man and actively so. *Vox dei, vox philosophi.*

This argument accords well with the notion of enlightenment philosophy as a radical improvement upon classical ambiguities. In particular, it is predicated upon the notion that the quest for truth about the human things can indeed eliminate the tension between law and justice, between convention and right. Accordingly, Rosso all but ignores Montesquieu's protracted dialogues with Plato-Socrates, entirely ignores those with Aristotle, and fails to mention Montesquieu's explicit expression of debt to Plato at least. In spite of the fact that this manifestly renders Montesquieu's philosophy less problematic—trivially so—it is not wholly misplaced.

Rosso emphasizes the "nozione tipica della problematica dei moralisti" addressed by Montesquieu. And that is the problem of willfulness, or intentionality. In Montesquieu this problem leads to an understanding of the fundamental nature of founding (and raises the question of differences in souls), but for Rosso it suffices to account for the full extent of Montesquieu's debt to Plato-Socrates. For it is these two great philosophers of antiquity "che Montesquieu doveva apprezzare almeno in quanto moralisti (e moralisti politici)." Montesquieu is one of the latter day moralists and thus owes to Plato-Socrates a great debt for having so influenced the goverments of their time and having constituted a basis for the moral authority of philosophy. Otherwise, Montesquieu has but "parole severe per it pensiero antico." In his own time geometry takes the place of Plato. Montesquieu is not Plato, "e i governati sono lontani dalla saggezza di Socrate."

According to this account, therefore, whatever tension may have existed between philosophy and politics was eliminated by Plato-Socrates. The triumph of philosophy eliminates the necessity for a judgment between the claims of philosophy and the claims of piety. That is, as philosophy becomes the sole standard of human morality, the philosophers are no longer subject to the charge of impiety. For the provenance of piety is nothing other than the Nietzschean will of that exalted personage, the philosopher. The danger to philosophy is removed by making philosophy the judge in a dispute to which philosophy is also a party. Such arrangements offend our sense of fairness. But the only other judge available is the polity itself—in our own time, democratic opinion. And the polity is also the other party to the dispute, having custody of piety. The alternatives are that one or the other may judge, or that both judge jointly. The practical difficulty of the later alternative imposes the necessity of choosing the former and justifying the claim of one party over the other. To Rosso, the manifestly superior wisdom of philosophy makes the choice easy.

It may be the case, however, that philosophy will refuse or be unable to speak to human morality save from the perspective of universal or cosmopolitan standards. And since human morality does not originally phrase itself in terms of universal standards, the appearance of philosophy's superior wisdom will have been acquired at the expense of concealing altogether the human claims. Hence, it may be unwise to defer completely to philosophy's judgment in a case to which philosophy is a party. Certainly, prior to confirming the superiority of philosophy, it would be necessary to express as forcefully as possible the claims of both parties to the dispute. Hence, philosophical morality, however understood, would have to be fully distinguished from political morality *before* they could be collapsed into a single principle of authority. Rosso fails to do this, but Montesquieu does not.

Philosophical morality, in its nature, binds but few men to men in general or in some particular city. Only a few can be philosophers (though philosophical morality, of course, can be applied to all if given the force of convention). But the few are bound as men and not as philosophers. This results in the notion that their being philosophers is a fact significant enough to warrant the expression of their human duties in a unique way. Yet, the duties remain human duties—in service of man or some men as opposed to philosophy as such.

Political morality, in its nature, binds all men to men in general or in some particular city. (The former case would especially represent the particular expression of that philosophical morality given the force of positive law, though that need not be the only example of a universal though closed horizon.) All men—including philosophers (who are neither beasts nor gods)—*must* live under the guidance of some regime, under politics and, hence, must encounter and practice the duties man owes to man.

Philosophy is incompatible with the mere practice of political morality, denying to it the very claim of comprehensiveness which is necessary to its existence. Yet, because political morality is comprehensive in a way that argument cannot refute (see above), philosophers, as men, must come to terms with it, with error. Uncontradicted universal opinion will always speak with greater authority than philosophy. Hence, it would seem that it is politics which must judge in its own case, though it is no more to be trusted to do so fairly than is philosophy.

If the mere practice of political morality is incompatible with philosophy, philosophers as philosophers must learn how to fulfill their duties as men from some philosophical morality. Philosophical morality has its origin in the necessity for philosophers to come to terms with political morality. And it is in service both of philosophy and politics, although in the case of the latter it is for the sake of the former.[10] The proper articulation of this fundamental ground of philosophy is the work of political philosophy.

It might be said that Montesquieu agrees with this account—and thus far is not a mere enlightenment philosopher—if his approaching the problem of human goodness through poetry (dialogue and fable) may be taken as a decisive indication. Rosso is certainly correct to focus far more attention on the fables than they have ever received before. But he is equally in error to remain under the sway of Shackleton's dictum. In opening his discussion of *Lysimaque* he points to the forceful defense of a supra-sensual human nature, founded in a love of virtue (para. 5). But he fails to reveal that the philosopher's concern at that point is to dissuade his friend from pushing too far his acquired love of courage. The lessons of virtue—at least for most—are to be applied in particular regimes. They are not to be generalized. Because Rosso ignores the drama of the dialogue—that is, he fails to take it seriously—he proceeds without inhibition to state "che la virtu e per Montesquieu essenzialmente 'aperture,' un moto affetivo che trascende it particolare e s'indirizza all'universale . . ." Now as to the philosopher, Callisthenes, this is in some measure true. But precisely to that extent is it also not true of men in general. And it is the purpose of this fable to reveal why this is so. But Rosso demonstrates, through this and other fables, precisely the opposite: that the philosopher's "transcendent openness" is *the* foundation of a philosophic morality, based in Montesquieu's "relativism," which may be prescribed for all men.

Rosso inquires no further into the *Lysimaque,* which is the principal source of Montesquieu's reflections on philosophical morality, but turns rather to the other fables, which principally discuss virtue in general or political morality. This seems defensible to him after he has achieved the collapsing of philosophical morality and political morality into the single term, virtue. And, following Montesquieu, this virtue is but a sentiment—directed to one's own good and the good of others ("estroversione o introversione del cuore")—which is founded on the love of pleasure. A sentiment is subject to nurture and control. But it is a matter of the heart—not the mind—and is therefore insusceptible to distinctions of true and false happiness (and, therefore, true and false pleasures?).

The control and nurture of the sentiments depend on the capacity to move the hearts of men—the appeal to their given passions. This is understood as the desire to enjoy pleasure in a peaceful harmony with others. Thus, the collapsing of philosophical morality into political morality eliminates the language of duty along with the pain endured for noble purposes. The virtue they become restates the political problem as a problem unrelated to philosophy as philosophy: "infatti non sono i filosofi coloro che turbano gli stati, ma quelli che non lo sono abbastanza per conoscere la loro felicita, e per godere." The hearts of citizens become subject to the science of nurturing proper sentiments because and only because social harmony depends upon "la critica del 'cœur'."

The only other mention of *Lysimaque* suggests the difficulty of Rosso's explanation. In a footnote he reflects that Montesquieu "persists" in an ethical judgment which regards, as "di una fatalità," natural and social components. To Rosso, this but creates the necessity to understand the social processes as imposing upon mankind an alienation from certain inner impulses—those natural components. Montesquieu calls this process self-renunciation, but he does not suggest that this political phenomenon is philosophical in nature. Man need not be understood as perfectible in Montesquieu's philosophy. Indeed, the speculative sciences render men unsociable precisely because they discourage self-renunciation. Rosso understands the problem entirely as a matter of baneful pride, requiring to be surpassed or subdued. Thus, politics usurps the role—political philosophy's role—of identifying the proper human souls or characters of soul. And the distinctions between souls are subordinated to the end of harmonious living in society. Hence, although this footnote recognizes Montesquieu's emphatic appreciation of differences in soul (a foundation without which the problem of philosophical morality cannot arise), it denies to that observation its philosophic as well as its political force. When Rosso observes, therefore, that one often notes in Montesquieu "il contrapunto fra 'grandes âmes' e 'petites âmes'," we conclude that he considers this one of the curiosities, the relics, of a philosophy whose soul is "il relativismo" which denies a place to "la 'purezza' e l''assolutezza' . . . nella vita dei sentimenti."

It is not an exaggeration to say that, by seizing upon the detailed prescription for modern regimes as the *foundation* of Montesquieu's philosophy, Rosso succeeds in narrowing Montesquieu's philosophy (in the same manner Plato's philosophy is narrowed by those who take the utopia of the *Republic* as the ultimate expression of Plato's purposes) and in fact subordinating its philosophical principles to mere political purpose. But there is no defense for that pursuit of political purpose apart from either the philosophy or some binding convention to which Montesquieu was subject. Montesquieu may indeed have become the "happiest of mortals" if he could have benefited mankind. But that desire could not have sprung from "la critica del cuore" which finds the problem of human welfare to be decisively political and not philosophical. This it is the burden of Montesquieu's moral fables to demonstrate.

In particular, the *Lysimaque* considers this question from the point of view of philosophical morality itself. Most of the other fables take the point of view of the city. For this very reason, though unconsciously, Rosso concentrates on the other fables. As a first step in developing Montesquieu's reconciliation of the tension between philosophical morality and political morality, a turn to the *Lysimaque* is appropriate. This turn to the *Lysimaque* as a source of Montesquieu's philosophical morality might be less defensible if it were indeed the case that no philosophical morality were developed or appropriate in *Esprit des Lois,* Montesquieu's comprehensive treatise on political philosophy. But he does in fact achieve such a statement there. This is not the place to develop that statement, but I wish to draw upon its basis as a foundation for the consideration of the *Lysimaque.*

The first eight books of *Esprit des Lois* are devoted primarily to an elaborate and artful consideration of the classical regime, and in particular to construction of the basis of that sentiment expressed in the *Pensées* that Plato's *Republic is* every bit as realizable as was the republic of

Sparta.[11] But this is almost to be expected, for Montesquieu says as well that his "système sur la liberté" must be understood in comparison with "les autres anciennes républiques."[12] He takes great pains to reveal this connection in *Esprit des Lois*. And those pains seem to have been entirely in service to the development of a philosophical morality. Montesquieu makes it clear that ancient political philosophy is the provenance of his chief interlocutor. (He never suggested that his system of liberty—*politique* was lined out in the manuscript—*must* be compared with modern philosophies.)

All of modern political philosophy prior to Montesquieu and at least after Rousseau has sought to offer an alternative to classical political philosophy but without demonstrating or attempting a defense of the alternative on the grounds of classical thought. It is Montesquieu's intention that his defense of the modern regime be understandable even from the perspective of classical political philosophy. To achieve this he advances the strongest possible argument for the classical alternative by showing that it is not only beautiful, but practically impossible. If, therefore, there is a particular ancient error upon which he concentrates, it is the reflection that the best regime were not practically possible.[13]

In Montesquieu's understanding, the ancients arrived at that conclusion because they wrongly identified the fundamental condition of that regime as the rule of philosophers—that is, the permanent holding of sovereign power by philosophers. Since that is politically impossible (and perhaps naturally impossible), they considered the utopia itself impossible. Now, it is not by accident that this circumstantial error of the ancients is also the fundamental objective of modern political philosophy, of the Enlightenment. By revealing the error of classical thought, Montesquieu undermines the assumptions of modern thought. Moderns, after all, developed principles which ultimately affirm the possibility of the utopia—thus agreeing with Montesquieu in rejecting the ancients. But utopia is to be achieved precisely by virtue of the fundamental condition or means eschewed by Montesquieu on the same grounds by which the ancients knew it to be impossible: enlightenment or the rule of philosophy.

What Montesquieu's critique means, then, is that the ancients failed to realize their dreams though they were best situated to do so, because they were insufficiently political. The paradox of the ancients is that they thought the realm of politics more limited than it in fact is. Hence, they envisioned no political alternative to philosopher-kings as such. The corresponding error of modern political philosophy is the idea that the realm of politics is truly unlimited. It is ignorant of the human ends. The moderns, much less favorably situated than the ancients, fail to realize their ambitions so long as, adopting the means they have, they reveal unconcern as to the end: so long as they are insufficiently philosophical.

The question as to what is the philosophical morality emerges as none other than, what is the golden mean for philosophy. Montesquieu's *Lysimaque* portrays at least one possibility. Consideration of it may reveal others. But in all events, if we may show that Montesquieu at some point sought to articulate the relationship between philosophers and sovereigns—whether one, few, or many—we may return to consideration of his contribution to the regime of modern liberalism with fewer qualms.

Lysimaque: **The Text**

After he had destroyed the Persian Empire, Alexander desired that men should consider him to be Jupiter's son. The Macedonian army was indignant to see this prince ashamed to have had Philip for a father; their discontent increased when they saw him assimilate the morals, habits, and manners of Persia; and they reproached themselves for having made so much of a man who now began to scorn them. But they only grumbled; no one spoke.

A philosopher, named Callisthenes, had accompanied the king on his expedition. Once, he saluted Alexander in the Greek manner. Whereupon the king demanded, "For what reason do you not worship me?" "Master," said Callisthenes, "You are commander to two nations: the one, slavish before you enslaved it, is no less so since your conquests. I am Greek, master, and you have so elevated that name that, without injuring you, I am no longer permitted to abase it."

Alexander's vices were extreme, as were his virtues; he was extreme in his anger, and it rendered him cruel. He ordered that Callisthenes' feet, nose, and ears be cut off, and that thus he should be carried in the army's train.

I loved Callisthenes, and always, when my tasks allowed some hours of leisure I employed them in listening to him. If I love virtue, I owe it to the impressions his discourse made on me. I went to see him. "I honor you." I told him, "Illustrious and unhappy one whom I see imprisoned like some wild beast in an iron cage, for having been the only man in the army."

"Lysimachus," he said, "when I am in a situation which demands strength and courage, it seems to me that I find myself almost at home. In truth, had the gods placed me on earth but to live a sensuous life, I would think that they had given me a great and immortal soul in vain. To enjoy sensual pleasure, that is a thing of which all men are easily capable; and, if the gods have only made us for that, they have produced a work more perfectly than they intended, and their work has been better completed than begun. It is not," he added, "that I am insensitive. You make me see only too well that I am not. When first you visited me here,

Lysimaque: **The Text**

Lorsqu'Alexandre eut détruit l'empire des Perses, il voulut que l'on crût qu'il étoit fils de Jupiter. Les Macédoniens étoient indignés de voir ce prince rougir d'avoir Philippe pour père: leur mécontentement s'accrut lorsqu'ils lui virent prendre les mœurs, les habits et les manières des Perses; et ils se reprochoient tous d'avoir tant fait pour un homme qui commençoit à les mépriser. Mais on murmuroit dans l'armée, & on ne parloit pas.

Un philosophe, nommé Callisthène, avait suivi le roi dans son expédition. Un jour qu'il le salua à la manière des Grecs: « D'où vient, lui dit Alexandre, que tu ne m'adores pas? » Seigneur, lui dit Callisthène, vous êtes chef de deux nations: l'une, esclave avant que vous l'eussiez soumise, ne l'est pas moins depuis que vous l'avez vaincue; l'autre, libre avant qu'elle vous servît à remporter tant de victoires, l'est encore depuis que vous les avez remportées. Je suis Grec, seigneur; & ce nom, vous l'avez élevé si haut, que, sans vous faire tort, il ne nous est plus permis de l'avilir. »

Les vices d'Alexandre étoient extrêmes comme ses vertus; il étoit terrible dans sa colère; elle le rendoit cruel. Il fit couper les pieds, le nez et les oreilles à Callisthène, ordonna qu'on le mît dans une cage de fer, & le fit porter ainsi à la suite de l'armée.

J'aimois Callisthène; &, de tout temps, lorsque mes occupations me laissaient quelques heures de loisir, je les avois employées à l'écouter; et si j'ai de l'amour pour la vertu, je le dois aux impressions que ses discours faisoient sur moi. J'allai le voir. « Je vous salue, lui dis-je, illustre malheureux, que je vois dans une cage de fer, comme on enferme une bête sauvage, pour avoir été le seul homme de l'armée. »

« Lysimaque, me dit-il, quand je suis dans une situation qui demande de la force & du courage, il me semble que je me trouve presque à ma place. En vérité, si les dieux ne m'avoient mis sur la terre que pour y mener une vie voluptueuse, je croirois qu'ils m'auroient donné en vain une âme grande et immortelle. Jouir des plaisirs des sens est une chose dont tous les hommes sont aisément capables; & si les dieux ne nous ont faits que pour cela, ils ont fait un ouvrage plus parfait qu'ils n'ont voulu & ils ont plus exécuté qu'entrepris. Ce n'est pas, ajouta-t-il, que je sois insensible. Vous ne me faites que trop voir que je ne le suis pas: quand

it was of some pleasure to watch you perform a courageous act. But, in the name of the gods, let this be the last time. Allow me to bear my misfortunes and do not be so cruel as to add to them further with your own."

"Callisthenes," I said, "I shall see you every day. If the king should see you abandoned by men of virtue, he would no longer be remorseful; he should begin to believe that you are guilty. Ah! I trust that he shall not enjoy the pleasure of seeing his punishments force me to abandon a friend."

One day Callisthenes said to me, "The immortal gods have consoled me; and since then I feel something divine within, which has relieved me of the thought of my pains. In a dream, I saw the great Jupiter. You were near to him and had a scepter in your hand, with a royal turban about your face. He showed you to me and said, 'He will make you happier.' The emotion that moved me woke me. I found myself, hands raised to heaven and trying to speak: 'Great Jupiter, if Lysimachus must reign, let him rule with justice.' Lysimachus, you will reign; believe a man who must find favor with the gods, since he suffers for virtue's sake."

Meanwhile, Alexander, having learned that I had respect for Callisthenes' misery, that I went to see him, and that I dared complain, was angered anew. "Go," he said, "combat the lions you unhappy soul, who finds pleasure in living so much among ferocious beasts." My sentence was deferred, in order that it might serve as a spectacle for a larger audience.

The day before, I wrote to Callisthenes in these words: "I go to die. The ideas of my future greatness, which you gave me, have fled my mind. I would have wanted to soften the ills of such as yourself."

Prexapias, in whom I had confided, brought this response to me: Lysimachus, if the gods have ordained that you should reign, Alexander can not take your life; men do not resist the will of the gods.

That letter encouraged me and, reflecting that happy and unhappy men are equally surrounded by the divine hand, I resolved to conduct myself, not by my hopes, but by my courage—to defend, until the end, a life in which there was such great promise.

vous êtes venu à moi, j'ai trouvé d'abord quelque plaisir à vous voir faire une action de courage; mais, au nom des dieux, que ce soit pour la dernière fois. Laissez-moi soutenir mes malheurs, et n'ayez point la cruauté d'y joindre encore les vôtres.»

« Callisthène, lui dis-je, je vous verrai tous les jours. Si le roi vous voyoit abandonné des gens vertueux, il n'auroit plus de remords: il commenceroit à croire que vous êtes coupable. Ah! j'espère qu'il ne jouira pas du plaisir de voir que ses châtiments me feront abandonner un ami. »

Un jour Callisthène me dit: « Les dieux immortels m'ont consolé; &, depuis ce temps, je sens en moi quelque chose de divin, qui m'a ôté le sentiment de mes peines. J'ai vu en songe le grand Jupiter. Vous étiez auprès de lui; vous aviez un sceptre à la main, & un bandeau royal sur le front. Il vous a montré à moi, & m'a dit: *Il te rendra plus heureux.* L'émotion où j'étois m'a réveillé. Je me suis trouvé les mains élevées au ciel, et faisant des efforts pour dire: *Grand Jupiter,* si *Lysimaque doit régner, fais qu'il règne avec justice.* Lysimaque, vous régnerez: croyez un homme qui doit être agréable aux dieux, puis-qu'il souffre pour la vertu. »

Cependant Alexandre ayant appris que je respectois la misère de Callisthène, que j'allois le voir, et que j'osois le plaindre, il entra dans une nouvelle fureur: « Va, dit-il, combattre contre les lions, malheureux qui te plais tant à vivre avec les bêtes féroces. » On différa mon supplice pour le faire servir de spectacle à plus de gens.

Le jour qui le précéda, j'écrivis ces mots à Callisthène « Je vais mourir. Toutes les idées que vous m'aviez données de ma future grandeur se sont évanouies de mon esprit. J'aurais souhaité d'adoucir les maux d'un homme tel que vous. »

Prèxape, à qui je m'étais confié, m'apporta cette réponse: « Lysimaque, si les dieux ont résolu que vous régniez, Alexandre ne peut pas vous ôter la vie; car les hommes ne résistent pas à la volonté des dieux.»

Cette lettre m'encouragea, &, faisant réflexion que les hommes les plus heureux & les plus malheureux sont également environnés de la main divine, je résolus de me conduire, non pas par mes espérances, mais par mon courage; & de défendre, jusqu'à la fin, une vie sur laquelle il y avait de si grandes promesses.

They brought me forth in a carriage, and I was surrounded by an immense throng which had come to witness either my courage or my fear. They released the lion. I had wrapped my arm with my coat, and this arm I offered him. He wanted to devour it. I seized his tongue, tore it from his mouth and threw him at my feet.

Alexander naturally loved courageous acts; he admired my resolution; and that moment was also the moment of the return of his great soul.

He summoned me and, offering his hand, said, "Lysimachus, I give you my friendship; give me yours. My anger has served only to make you perform an act which is missing in Alexander's life."

I received the king's graces, worshipped the decrees of the gods, and awaited their promises without either pursuing or fleeing them. Alexander died, and the world was without a master. The king's sons were in their nonage; his brother Arideus had never left it. Olympia only had the hardiness of weak souls and, for her, all that was cruel was courage. Roxanne, Eurydice, and Statyra were lost to sadness. In the palace, everyone knew how to moan and no one knew how to rule. Then, Alexander's captains cast their eyes upon the throne, but the ambition of each was checked by the ambition of all. We divided the empire, and each of us also believed he shared the prize of his efforts.

Fate made me king of Asia and, now that my will is everything, I have greater need than ever of the lessons of Callisthenes. His joy informs me that I have done some good, and his sighs tell me that I have some wrong to repair. I find him between me and my people.

I am king of a people who love me. Fathers of families wish, for me, a long life—as they do for their children; children fear to lose me, as they fear to lose their fathers. My subjects are happy, and so am I.

End

On me mena dans la carrière. Il y avait autour de moi un peuple immense qui venait être témoin de mon courage ou de ma frayeur. On me lâcha un lion. J'avais plié mon manteau autour de mon bras: je lui présentai ce bras: il voulut le dévorer: je lui saisis la langue, la lui arrachai, et le jettai à mes pieds.

Alexandre aimait naturellement les actions courageuses: il admira ma résolution; & ce moment fut celui du retour de sa grande âme.

Il me fit appeler; et me tendant la main: « Lysimaque, me dit-il, je te rends mon amitié, rends-moi la tienne. Ma colère n'a servi qu'à te faire faire une action qui manque à la vie d'Alexandre. »

Je reçus les grâces du roi. J'adorai les décrets des dieux; & j'attendois leurs promesses, sans les rechercher ni les fuir. Alexandre mourut; & toutes les nations furent sans maître. Les fils du roi étoient dans l'enfance: son frère Aridée n'en étoit jamais sorti: Olympias n'avoit que la hardiesse des âmes foibles, et tout ce qui étoit cruauté étoit pour elle du courage: Roxane, Eurydice, Statyre, étoient perdues dans la douleur. Tout le monde, dans le palais, sçavoit gémir; & personne ne sçavoit régner. Les capitaines d'Alexandre levèrent donc les yeux sur son trône: mais l'ambition de chacun fut contenue par l'ambition de tous. Nous partageâmes l'empire; et chacun de nous crut avoir partagé le prix de ses fatigues.

Le sort me fit roi d'Asie; & à présent que je puis tout, j'ai plus besoin que jamais des leçons de Callisthène. Sa joie m'annonce que j'ai fait quelque bonne action; et ses soupirs me disent que j'ai quelque mal à réparer. Je le trouve entre mon peuple et moi.

Je suis le roi d'un peuple qui m'aime. Les pères de famille espèrent la longueur de ma vie, comme celle de leurs enfants: les enfants craignent de me perdre comme ils craignent de perdre leur père. Mes sujets sont heureux, et je le suis.

Fin

Commentary

(Para. 1) The sovereign (tyrant) aspires to divinity, whether by nature or by circumstance is not said. But, among men, the recognition of divinity requires distance from the human things. "Morals, habits, and manners" all contrive to produce an image of divinity, by which standard men judge even gods themselves—our gods, their gods. The tyrant's aspiration is to universalize men in their moral sentiments. As such, his aspiration conflicts both with the universal aspiration of philosophy to comprehend human goodness and with the aspiration of the city. The aspiration of the city—of human morality—is to distinguish itself from other cities. (Para. 2) Yet; only the philosopher will challenge the tyrant's universal aspirations. He does so, however, not in the name of philosophy but in the name of some city. If he, too, aspires to divinity, must he do so as a citizen? Callisthenes' standards are not merely parochial, for he may oppose even the sovereign in the name of the sovereign's own good. But this particular sovereign is a tyrant. That Callisthenes should oppose even Alexander in the name of the city suggests that the city is not coincident with the tyrant's will. Or, the law that is made is made pursuant to an end, which end alone is that to which the philosopher gives loyalty. (Para. 3) But the sovereign alone both speaks in the name of the city and gives motion to the city. Hence, the philosopher's loyalty to the "true" city is insufficient, politically, when he has business with the tyrant. And he has no apparent recourse but to suffer penalties, since he can be no further political (interrupt the quest for truth for the sake of moral goodness) than is consistent with the political activity the "true" city would demand.

(Para. 4) Lysimachus, the narrator, now speaks in his own name. But what he has already said in his narration introduces him. He was among the grumbling captains who never spoke. He silently witnesses, first, the bravery, and, then, the "cruel" punishment of Callisthenes. And he is aware of Alexander's extreme cholers. Now, when he reports that he has long been nurtured in conversations by Callisthenes and taught to love virtue, we can wonder if that virtue were the virtue of the good citizen in the "true city" or the prudent silence he has already manifested. That is, did Callisthenes teach him the importance of ruling and being ruled in turn, simply, or did he teach him to rule himself by the standard of the "true" city? Upon visiting and honoring Callisthenes, now an outcast, Lysimachus reveals that he does have some standard beyond convention. He tells the philosopher that he was the "only man in the army." Lysimachus recognizes a standard of manliness which may not of necessity conflict with the actual city but is indeed independent of it. By honoring his manliness, he exits his silence and approaches manliness himself. (Para. 5) Callisthenes reminds Lysimachus that Callisthenes' supra-political courage is natural to himself in the same way that his freedom from enslavement to the passions is natural. It is as much required for the pursuit of the ends of a "great and immortal soul." It is true, however, that all men are endowed with these contrary faculties of the soul. Yet, Lysimachus must not act in respect to them as Callisthenes himself does. The philosopher derives pleasure from his contemplation of the effort a lesser soul makes to perform a courageous act, but it is still more necessary to remind Lysimachus to measure his activity by something more solid. Hence, he is implored "in the name of the gods" to avoid a misfortune for which he is not prepared. The gods, that is, are given to Lysimachus as a means of counsel less rigorous than the demands of philosophy, yet still higher than mere passion or aversion to pain. He is solicited not by an appeal to his self-interest, but by the combined and related appeals to the gods and his love of the philosopher as distinct from philosophy.

(Para. 6) This combined appeal proves insufficient to restrain a soul charmed by supra-political courage. Lysimachus now knows that there is a nobility to which he can aspire which does not depend on the pleasure of the tyrant. Hence, he must remind Callisthenes that, having liberated his own soul from the fear of pain, Lysimachus can no longer govern himself by the injuries his lovers would feel at the sight of pain to himself. He now acts for the sake of virtue—a virtue opposed to the tyrant's strength—and to demonstrate to Alexander the superior strength of philosophic friendship. If Callisthenes had undertaken his counsel to prudence seriously, he must adopt a new strategy. The ambition for greatness that has arisen in the soul of Lysimachus can no longer be moderated by such counsel of itself. (Para. 7) Callisthenes again invokes the gods. This time, however, they have spoken to him. He does not make a prayer in their name, but rather reports a statement directly from Jupiter, the same Jupiter by whom Alexander wished to have been fathered. The god indirectly assures Callisthenes and Lysimachus that Lysimachus will survive his daring act. But he does so by foreseeing the consummation of Lysimachus' ambition—thereby revealing the true nature of that ambition. More directly, Jupiter provides—through Callisthenes—an object for that ambition and, in doing so, transforms the courage from the supra-political to the political. Awakened from his dream, the philosopher addresses the god directly, counseling him to permit Lysimachus to rule "with justice." The ambition is enlarged. Lysimachus will not be a mere tyrant; hence he must seek not only power, but knowledge how to use it.

(Para. 8) Lysimachus completely blossoms. No longer among the silent, he now "complains" of Alexander's cruelty. This brings the expected royal reward: a sentence of death. But it is not merely death; it is rather to be death in the form of a challenge to that very courage which initiated the offense and before his fellow citizens, hence a challenge to the ambition for honor which accompanied the courage. (Para. 9) This sentence accomplishes what Callisthenes' initial counsel could not. May it have been a test? Lysimachus finds he had set his sights too high. The price he must pay is to sacrifice the pleasures which were within his reach. Now that his mind no longer entertains "ideas of my future greatness," it must rather settle upon the fear of death and the pleasures of the body death interrupts. He does not now remember his wish to teach Alexander a lesson; he only wished to minimize the pains of Callisthenes.

(Para. 10) Callisthenes responds, neither in the name of the gods nor as a messenger from Jupiter, but as the authoritative interpreter of the gods. What exists by will of the gods may not be thwarted by human will. Hence, Lysimachus need reflect neither upon ideas of future greatness nor upon imminent pains. He need only cultivate those faculties required to serve the end which has already been made manifest to him. Alexander's challenges become the occasion for Lysimachus to merit his destiny. It is a sufficient goal for the generality of men to wish to deserve the good things they may obtain. By the point of this exchange of notes, Lysimachus has been completely transformed. His desire for a transpolitical good has been encouraged. (Para. 11) His victory is specifically a demonstration of courage rather than fear, but it is a courage which is unrelated to the fear of pain. (Para. 12) Alexander recognizes the act as proceeding from a greatness of soul. Its kinship with his own soul overcomes his anger. Lysimachus has learned to move himself as the tyrant moves himself, but without the eros for divinity. (Para. 13) Friendship with the tyrant—the fitting reward for the specific act—supplants friendship with the philosopher. The tyrant's friend may always perform an act which participates in the essence of tyranny and which may nonetheless elude the tyrant himself. The philosopher's friend may only participate in a common achievement.

(Para. 14) Lysimachus enters into the tyrant's friendship, but now follows counsels of prudence. He avoids the trap of Macbeth, perhaps because he is himself counseled by an interpreter of the gods who is as much concerned with men as with divine things. But, upon the king's death, Lysimachus and his fellow captains struggle for the empire, and content themselves to divide it. Lysimachus was not loath to fight to realize the decree of the gods—once the tyrant was gone. The prudent counsel he followed must have borne some relation to the nature of the tyranny or the particular tyrant. Guiding himself now by political rather than transpolitical ideas or ambitions, he is capable of distinguishing the relationship of political events to political opportunities. He becomes a statesman. But, still he carries with him a decree of the gods which pre-exists the regime he creates. (Para. 15) In Lysimachus' mind it is rather fate than choice that made him "king of Asia." Hence, his desires can not be the basis of his attaining or exercising power. Yet, his "will is everything." He has, in other words, everything the completely erotic man requires but the eros. He must, therefore, possess a substitute. The substitute is Callisthenes. The philosopher provides him measures of good and evil merely by smiling or frowning upon his actions. That is, through the manifest pleasures or pains Callisthenes takes in the contemplation of Lysimachus' actions Lysimachus can judge the rightness of his actions. The standard of political goodness is the pleasure or eros of the philosopher. But the philosopher seems to take his bearing from the common good—the good of the people. Hence, he mediates the people's desires for the prince and makes these mediated or purged desires the desires of the prince himself. We remember that he also mediated the desires of the gods for the prince. Since the gods are the declared source of the only genuine desire Lysimachus has, the desires of the gods are as much mediated or purged as those of the people. Does the philosopher dare to speak the truth to this prince? Yes, if only because this prince can have no ambition which is not sanctioned by the erotic prophet. As this prince has a freedom from eros, this regime has a freedom from religion.

(Para. 16) The philosopher disappears. But the work he has created remains. There is now a king and his people, and both are happy. They may owe their happiness to Callisthenes, but the people at least are unaware of this. They only honor their king. The king receives the honor bestowed upon him as if he merited it himself. And is he not just? He enjoys it, after all, not because Callisthenes taught him how to attain it but rather because Jupiter fated him to attain it and he possessed the character of soul which allowed him to exert himself in order to deserve it. To Lysimachus, the philosopher's pleasure may be a necessary cause of the justice of his rule, but it is not a sufficient cause. Lysimachus perceives no problem in Callisthenes' relationship to Jupiter. To Lysimachus, Callisthenes is only a prophet. The philosopher's ambition for the divine ceases to be a political problem when the philosopher becomes the only genuine prophet, which he becomes when he acts under the necessity of substituting his eros for that of the ruler. In doing so, he removes, by means of political prudence, the foundation for the tyrant's challenge to his claim of supra-political loyalty. The final words of the dialogue become especially weighty. "My subjects are happy, and so am I."[14] The work of philosophy is to provide for the happiness of the sovereign as well as that of the governed.[15] But, in this regime, is the philosopher himself happy? The question does not arise. Can that mean it would be inappropriate to raise such a question in this context? Is the happiness of the philosopher to be judged only on the basis of those activities engendered by his supra-political loyalties? If that were so, we could say at the least that, in this regime, we have occasion to consider the happiness of the philosopher. It remains a question, although the conditions which would permit leisurely consideration of the question impose a positive duty upon the philosopher. To search for his own happiness, the philosopher must address the happiness of men—and that politically rather than philosophically.

Conclusion

We can now attempt a summary of the implications of this dialogue. Contending that knowledge is indeed virtue, Montesquieu accounts for the difficulties emanating from that conception which concerned Aristotle.[16] The chief difficulty seemed to be that the knower must rule for goodness to prevail. To show that that is not required, Montesquieu elaborates that philosophical morality which responds to Lowenthal's search. Though maintaining that knowledge is virtue, Montesquieu discloses that knowledge itself—in the person of the knower—may suffer at the hands of human affairs as much as virtue itself may suffer when left to the care of the mute elements.[17] It is precisely because naked knowledge possesses no means of defense that a philosophical morality is presented in the form of a moral fable. This is revealed in the most famous of the moral fables.

Montesquieu commences his myth of the "Troglodytes" with an apology. The tale is a moral fable, and he indicates that moral fables must be justified. Although the tale is in the mouth of Usbek, in *Les Lettres Persans,* it is yet necessary to distinguish between philosophic tales and moral tales. Usbek's disclaimer maintains the preeminence of friendship to reason in a discussion of moral matters. The story of the Troglodytes is intended to prove that one cannot be happy but by practicing virtue. Such a lesson seems to be properly the preserve of political philosophy. But philosophy, Montesquieu suggests, cannot fully persuade. Usbek commences his tale.

Il y a de certaines vérités qu'il ne suffit pas de persuader, mais qu'il faut encore faire sentir; telles sont les vérités de morale. Peut-être que ce morceau d'histoire te touchera plus qu'une philosophie subtile.

Of certain truths it does not suffice to persuade, but it is further necessary to make one feel; such are the truths of morality. Perhaps this morsel of history will engage you more than a subtle philosophy.

Among the moral fables one finds Montesquieu dealing with one of the principal tenets of his teaching: the necessity to preserve the sphere of practical wisdom in a world increasingly coming to be dedicated to theoretical wisdom. The treatment Callisthenes received at the hands of Alexander depicts the urgency of such a consideration.

Montesquieu has liberally rewritten the historical evidence. It is disputed whether Callisthenes was mutilated or simply executed. It is doubtful whether he were so sober as depicted,[18] and it is uncertain whether Lysimachus were a student of his. The tale must be taken then in terms of the changes that have been made but only as those changes reveal some element of the art involved in its construction. Though Montesquieu rewrites the history, in choosing one of Alexander's Captains to memorialize, he reveals a standard. He constructs the history on the possible fact that Lysimachus—of all the successors—alone failed to launch an aggressive war in the struggle over the spoils of the empire. His share falls to him in some measure by chance. On the other hand, he never hesitated to join alliances and move aggressively in his own defense, and he always seemed to cover his own aggrandizing intentions as a response to a plausible threat. His actions, therefore, reveal fully that political ambition which animates the tyrant at the same time they disclose an uncertainty as to the legitimacy of those ambitions.

Such a soul, which may actually exist, is the natural ally of the philosopher in the attempt to erect a good regime. The one thing that soul lacks is certainty. The certainty can be provided by philosophy, provided the philosopher does not attempt to inculcate philosophic certainty. For that will enlarge the original ambition. Can it be that Montesquieu, too, blames Aristotle for the dimensions and significance of Alexander's conquests? That certainty which should be provided is the dependence of human goodness upon divine will.

The gods speak of and to statesmen through philosophers. Divine wisdom intervenes in human affairs only through philosophic wisdom. There can appear no conflict between reason and revelation, if the condition for receiving revelation is philosophic openness. Hence, the statesman will realize that, to the extent he receives revelation from a philosopher, he is a child of philosophy. His "idea of greatness" will be philosophic conceptions which he receives upon trust. He will not judge those conceptions by any standard beyond prudent experience. But even in this he is limited. The philosopher reminds him of the divine origin of the "ideas of greatness." No mundane experience—however dramatic—can challenge the truthfulness of the heavenly *logos*. To fail to follow the philosopher's dream is not to cease to believe in philosophy but to cease to believe in god.[19]

That Lysimachus's lapsarianism is aborted by these reflections is due entirely to the connection of this argument with his ambition, which, in its precise form, has also been imparted. The slaying of the lion becomes identical with winning the Asian kingdom. Both are assigned to fate, but fate or chance, we see, is the prudent exercise of favored ambitions. His ambition is to be able to do anything, but its realization forces him to seek what to do. Only the perfect human being can know what to will. The statesman is imperfect for he remains dependent upon earthly honor.[20] That is, in wishing to will all, he reveals that those things which are the objects of will constitute his highest ambitions. Those things have to do with pleasures and pains and, as such, are inferior to the true purpose or end of the "great and immortal soul." Yet, this last alone can properly answer the question as to what should be willed; in virtue of its superiority to though not detachment from (notice Callisthenes's misery!) those ambitions. Because Callisthenes stands between Lysimachus and god—the place of highest human honor—he mediates between Lysimachus and the people; he becomes the standard of earthly honor. The philosopher is higher than the statesman—yet unnoticed by the people.

For that which the people honor is not that whereby philosophy is honored.[21] Callisthenes stands between Lysimachus and the people only to the extent that the statesman learns from the philosopher—his counselor—of the people's requirements. The philosopher in that relationship is of less dignity than the statesman, and hence unseen—and unloved—by the people. Yet, insofar as his wisdom is the condition both of the sovereign's ambitions and of the people's love for the sovereign, the people love, unknowingly, philosophy. If Rousseau is correct, that philosophy cannot be democratized and must be essentially unknown to be safe, and if philosophy must be loved and worshipped to thrive;[22] then Montesquieu has propounded a philosophical morality which ties philosophy to the happiness of the good regime without enslaving philosophy to the passions of the many. He does so by rendering philosophers politically the most important and least honored of the citizens of the good regime.[23] But from their service, philosophers derive the greatest good.

Notes

1. In honor of Leo Strauss' contribution to modern philosophy, this essay is dedicated to Harry V. Jaffa. It was previously published in the *Independent Journal of Philosophy,* vol. ii (1978): 71-80.

2. Robert Shackleton, *Montesquieu: A Critical Biography* (London: Oxford University Press, 1961). He accounts for the *Lysimaque* strictly as a bit of romantic poetry addressed to the exiled King Stanislas of Poland: "He did not visit the Polish court again, but he wrote for it the last work which he published during his lifetime. This was *Lysimaque, a* short prose narrative of which *the idea had occurred to him twenty years before [Pensée,* 563 (Barckhausen. 439)].* Reminiscent of his *Dialogue de Sylla et d Eucrate* for the style, and of the story of the Troglodytes for the theme, it has an allegorical substructure applicable to the exiled Polish monarch, for it described the eventual triumph over a capricious despot of an enlightened ruler who was the friend of a philosopher." (Emphasis added) I maintain that the *Lysimaque* may well have served this function without, thereby, being limited to the expression of puerile sentiments. Shackleton, too, may have appreciated this had he given sufficient emphasis to the underscored portion above, which reveals that Montesquieu had conceived the fable some twenty years before the occasion to court Stanislas had arisen. Indeed, precisely to the extent that doing public honor to a king is undertaken seriously must one endeavor to do so fittingly. And if there is, further, some

question as to what the nature of the relationship between a philosopher and a ruler should be, any essay by a philosophical courtier must bear the burden of respecting or at least elucidating that relationship in terms and manner destructive of the self-esteem of neither kings nor philosophers. In the analysis that follows I think it emerges plainly that no philosopher as such can be merely a courtier.

3. David Lowenthal, "Montesquieu and the Classics," in Joseph Cropsey, ed., *Ancients and Moderns* (New York: Basic Books, 1964). What is critical in Lowenthal's account is the identification of "philosophical virtue" with "philosophical morality," which produces the awkward circumstance that "philosophical virtue . . . is politically harmful" in spite of the fact that the philosopher, as natural legislator, is determined to benefit mankind by a "philosophical morality" (p. 281). Another way of saying this is that the first moralist is the philosopher, and the first enemy of his work is himself. It is possible that this is true. But it is also likely that an intolerable tension exists between the two terms of this expression. See 3-10 above and note 9 below.

4. Note the substantive difference between this formulation and Shackleton's argument that the *Lysimaque* "described the eventual triumph over a capricious despot of an enlightened ruler who was the friend of a philosopher."

5. See note 9.

6. Thomas Pangle, *Montesquieu's Philosophy of Liberalism* (Chicago: University of Chicago Press, 1973); W. B. Allen, *Montesquieu: The Federalist-Antifederalist Dispute,* Phd. diss. (Claremont: Claremont Graduate School, 1972).

7. W.B. Allen, "Theory and Practice in the Founding of the Republic," *Interpretation,* vol. IV, no. 2, 1974, 79-97.

8. Cf. my review of Pangle's "Montesquieu," *Journal of the History of Philosophy*, vol. XIII, no. 2, April, 1975, 256-259; also, see James Madison's unacknowledged use of Montesquieu's *Considerations on the Causes of the Greatness of the Romans and of Their Decline*, Ch. III; in *Federalist Papers*, no. 43.

9. Corrado Rosso, *Montesquieu Moralista: Dalle leggi al "bonheur"* (Pisa: Editrice Libreria Goliardica, 1965). Cf., especially, the opening paragraph at 63 and the chapter on virtue from 187 to 197.

10. Philosophic morality is not the same as philosophic politics, which eventuate in *Republics*. Cf. Leo Strauss, *On Tyranny* (Ithaca: Cornell University Press, 1968), 220. "Plato could not have decided, however provisionally, in favor of the Spartan regime, if the philosopher's concern with a good political order were absolutely inseparable from the concern guiding his philosophic politics. In what then does philosophic politics consist? In satisfying the city that the philosophers are not atheists . . . but good citizens and even the best of citizens. This is the defense of philosophy which was required always and ev-

erywhere, whatever the regime might have been. For, as the philosopher, Montesquieu, says, 'dans tous les pays du monde, on veut de la morale' and 'les hommes, fripons en detail, sont en gros de trés honnêtes gens; ils aiment la morale.' This defense of philosophy before the tribunal of the city was achieved by Plato with a resounding success (Plutarch, *Nicias*, ch. 23). The effects have lasted down to the present throughout all ages except the darkest ones."

11. Montesquieu, *Pensées,* no. 1208 (no. 1811, Barckhausen edn.), Edition Nagel, 1950.

12. *Pensées,* no. 907 (no. 80, Barckhausen).

13. See the critique of Aristotle at Bk. V, ch. 8, and the chapter as a whole in its context.

14. Strauss, *On Tyranny* 70-71, "The Teaching Concerning Tyranny": "The correction of tyranny consists in nothing else than the transformation of the unjust or vicious tyrant who is more or less unhappy into a virtuous tyrant who is happy. As for the tyrant's subjects, or his city, Simonides makes it clear that it may be very happy. The tyrant and his subjects may be united by bonds of natural kindness." We must remember that the word "law" is never mentioned in the *Lysimaque*.

15. Op. cit., Strauss, "The Two Ways of Life," 88-89. "The specific function of the ruler appears to be strictly subordinate to that of the wise man. In the best case imaginable, the ruler would be the one who, by means of honoring, to say nothing of punishing, would put into practice the teaching or the prescriptions of the wise man. The wise man is the ruler of rulers." Whether by "best case imaginable" Strauss means the "best in fact" is uncertain. But he does remind the reader of the notion of a philosopher-king when he shows Xenophon's agreement with Plato-Socrates as to the logical necessity of understandig the ruler, in the strict sense, as the knower. Hence, when he speaks generically of the "wise man" as the "ruler of rulers," his account of Xenophon approaches Montesquieu for as long as we do not conceive the expression, "ruler of rulers," to include a reference to the self-rule of the philosopher-king. That this last is not likely we conceive, again, when Strauss adds, "The wise man sits leisurely upon the very good toward which the ruler is blindly and furiously working his way and which he will never reach."

16. *Nicomachean Ethics*, Bk. I; *Politics*, Bk. III, Ch. IV.

17. See *Esprit des Lois*, Bks. XII to XIX, but especially Bks. XIV to XIX.

18. For a general account of Callisthenes and Lysimachus, see Charles Rollin, *The Ancient History,* translated from the French (New York: American Book Exchange, 1880).

19. Op. cit., Strauss, "Piety and Law," 107. "Divine approval and divine assistance *seem* to be indispensable for salutary political action." (Emphasis added.)

20. Laurence Berns, "Gratitude, Nature, and Piety in King Lear," *Interpretation,* vol. 3, no. 1, 33, n. 21. Note, in Jaffa's account, the similarity between Lear's confused challenge to Cordelia and Alexander's open confrontation of Callisthenes in the account above.

21. Anthony, Earl of Shaftesbury, *Characteristics of Men, Manners, Opinions, Times,* "A Letter Concerning Enthusiasm" (New York: Bobbs-Merrill Co., [1964]), 27-30. See especially the final two paragraphs of Section IV and all of Section V. Shaftesbury reflects on the paradox that the deserved praise of what is good can only be affected by him that has mastered the good. Montesquieu did not necessarily consult Shaftesbury in writing the *Lysimaque,* but he was familiar with him. He speaks, in *Pensée,* 1092 (2095, Barckhausen edn.), of "milord Shaftesbury" as one of "les quatre grands poètes." The other three are Malebranche, Montaigne, and Plato. Montesquieu's appreciation of Shaftesbury may be reflected in his judgment of ancient philosophy as having rendered men savage or unsociable *(Esprit des Lois,* IV, 8). In Shaftesbury's terms, the criticism would rather be of an impolitic philosophy than philosophy itself. "A mannerly wit can hurt no cause or interest for which I am in the least concerned; and philosophical speculations, politely managed, can never surely render mankind more unsociable or uncivilised." Cf., "Freedom of Wit and Humor," Part II, Sec. III. This is perhaps the intent of Thomas More's response to Hythlodaeus in *Utopia,* Bk. I, when he maintains that a "jarring," "tragicomic" philosophy is insufficiently "polite" or "urbane" to be introduced into the councils of kings. But by refusing to consider himself a philosopher, More reveals uncertainty as to the consequences for philosophy of such politic—pre-philosophic—methods. Montesquieu's Callisthenes is more complicated. Being made less obnoxious that historically reputed, Callisthenes is provided the character of indirection recommended by More. But, because Montesquieu's philosopher refuses to countenance falsehood and lying, he more nearly approaches the intent of Machiavelli's "unless men are compelled to be good, they will invariably turn out evil." At the end of the 23rd chapter of the *Prince,* of course, Machiavelli seems to rejoin rule and wisdom. Hence, a prince's truthful advisors will speak to a man genuinely their equal or better. This is emphasized strongly in the statement that a prince who delivers himself into the hands of a wise man will soon be supplanted by him. Philosophers do indeed possess the character of soul required for tyrannical ambition, according to Machiavelli. So far is this the case, that a wise prince must compel his advisors to obey the demands of philosophical virtue. Such an advisor would be ruled rather by the prince than his own wisdom. Since More's and Machiavelli's conflicting demands seem to be united in Montesquieu's account, Montesquieu must not agree that it is necessary to unite philosophical and political power. Only by denying this can he still maintain that the goodness of the ruler has its source in the wisdom of the philosopher. But that is what reveals the difficulty of this account: The circumstances of philosophical morality are such that the philoso-

pher can have recourse neither to force nor to the noble lie in order to pursue human goodness.

22. Alexandre Kojeve, "Tyranny and Wisdom," in Strauss, *On Tyranny,* 170-172, where Kojeve questions the ultimate detachment of the philosopher. "Now, as long as a man is alone in knowing something, he can never be sure that he truly knows it . . . It is impossible to know whether the philosopher (wise man) seeks knowledge and practices virtue 'for themselves' (or 'out of duty') or whether he does it for the sake of the 'pleasure' (joy) he derives from doing so, or—finally—whether he acts in this way in order to feel admiration for himself (conditioned or not by admiration on the part of others)." It is perhaps an accident that this axiom of modern philosophy coincides perfectly with the superordination of political virtue to philosophical virtue that we found in Machiavelli. Reconsider Strauss' "The Two Ways of Life," and the difference between love and honor.

23. Cf. Kojeve; I do not know that Kojeve was correct, but it remains the case that if the philosopher is to substitute his eros for that of the tyrant (or government) whether from the need (or desire) for students or from a sense of duty—he must still contend with the difficulty that his wisdom, in itself, is not susceptible to the kind of praise required by political health (or philosophical opportunity).

Chapter 3

Montesquieu's *Sulla and Eucrates*

Translation and Commentary

Preface

The dialogue between Sulla and Eucrates reminds of nothing so force-fully as it reminds of Xenophon's similar dialogue between Hiero and Simonides. Doubtless, therefore, we approach it best by distinguishing Montesquieu's dialogue from that of his model. For Xenophon, where the tyrant, Hiero, bore the name of an historical actor (Hiero of Syracuse) just as Montesquieu's Sulla bears the name of the Roman Sulla, his Simonides bears the name of the historical poet, while Montesquieu's Eucrates is fictive, not a poet, and might be taken to derive from Plato's "philosopher king." For his name means good or happy ruler, and he has no historical antecedent apart from the fiction of the *Republic*. "Eucrates" does not appear in Nails's *The People of Plato*.[1] However, when Socrates completes the founding of the best constitution, he explicitly says it may bear the name either of "basileia" or of "aristokratia." (*Republic*, 445d)

"Eucrates" is the name of the founder of the best "city in speech," and therefore especially well suited to question a Sulla who imagines himself a founder. By contrast, Simonides is the name of a real poet—a maker of fictions—who is credited in *Republic* with authoring a false definition of justice as paying back what is due. Simonides, who had a reputation for wisdom, sought out Hiero to inquire whether tyrants are differently happy from ordinary men. That is, Xenophon's poet needed yet to inquire about happiness from someone reputed or supposed to be in a position to know. Montesquieu opened "Sulla" with the dictator, Sulla, seeking out the philosopher on account of the philosopher's reputation. That is, Montesquieu's dictator seemed not to know the answer to the question raised by Simonides (whether personal and political happiness are the same or different) but imagined to find an answer from a philosopher.

Moreover, Montesquieu's Sulla imagines himself no tyrant, whereas Hiero knows that he is "merely" a tyrant (i.e., he has no awareness of the private citizen apart from the tyrant's will). The historical Sulla sought to save Rome, and Montesquieu's fictional recreation insists that his doing so made him merely the first citizen in Rome. He quit his power to resume his private situation, on the belief that he preferred the enjoyments of private life to the power of public life. Yet, he longs to know whether he has done well publicly, and whether he can dwell in safety as a private citizen, having acted as he did publicly.

Eventually, the discussion between Hiero and Simonides highlights the differences between the tyrant and the poet, the public and the private man, and discloses them competitors for the greatest happiness independent of public happiness.[2] The discussion between Sulla and Eucrates, therefore, may well reveal whether there is happiness independent of public happiness. It helps in conceiving how to read this dialog to remember two things: first, Montesquieu has already published *Lysimaque* before he published *Sulla*. Thus, a certain form of the relation of the tyrant and the philosopher has already been elaborated—namely, the relation of counsel or adviser. Second, Sulla is perhaps the only fictive character about whom Montesquieu has written more extensively in his historical oeuvre than in his fictional oeuvre. Accordingly, the ultimate judgment of *Sulla* must invoke the historical account that flowed from the same pen, in order to discern the teaching peculiarly associated with the fictional account.

In Book VI, Chapter 15 of his *Esprit des lois,* Montesquieu wrote, "I feel secure in my maxims when I have the Romans with me." He seemed in this to mean that he validates the philosophical principles he deduced from political practice by testing the principles against Roman experience. That orientation is reflected not only in his initial historical discussion of Rome (*Considerations*) but throughout *Esprit des lois,* in which we find the turn to Rome recurring regularly after each major elaboration of deductive principles. *Sulla* is a fable devoted to giving a character portrait of the famous Roman General and Consul, and it is the only *historical* fable in the collection of fables. To provide a commentary on the fable, therefore, a reader must first consult those expository accounts of Sulla that appear in the philosophical treatises. Accordingly, the "Commentary" shall consist of the translated excerpts from the *Esprit des Lois* (A) and the *Considerations* (B), following which an interpretive conclusion will close this section.

Sulla and d'Eucrates:[3] **The Text**

A few days after Sulla had quitted the dictatorship, I learned that the reputation that I had among philosophers caused him to wish to see me. He was at his Tiber estate, where he was enjoying the first quiet moments of his life. I did not feel before him that disorder which the presence of the great ordinarily induces in us. And from the moment we were alone, I said to him, "So, Sulla, is it you who have placed yourself in that condition of mediocrity which afflicts nearly all humans? You have renounced that authority that your glory and your virtues procured for you over all men? Fortune seems to have been hobbled, no longer to elevate you to honors."

"Eucrates," he said to me, "if I am no longer a spectacle to the universe, it is the fault of the human things, which suffer limits, and not mine. I thought I had fulfilled my destiny from that moment I no longer had great things to do. I was not made to govern quietly a slavish people. I love to conquer, to found or to destroy states, to form alliances, to punish the usurper. But, as for the petty details of government where mediocre minds have so many advantages; that slow execution of the laws, that command of a tranquil militia; my soul does not know how to pursue such things."

"It is singular," I told him, "that you should have brought such fine distinctions [squeamishness] to ambition. Many are the great men we have seen little moved by the vain glitter and pomp which surrounds those who govern, but few are they who have not been sensitive to the pleasure of governing and of commanding at their whim that respect which is due only to the laws."

"And I, Eucrates," he told me, "I have never been so little happy as when I saw myself the absolute master in Rome, as when I have looked about me and found neither rivals nor enemies.

"I believed that people would some day say that I had only punished slaves. 'Do you want,' I asked myself, 'that there should no longer be in your country any men who could be touched by your glory? And, since you established the tyranny, do you not very well see that there will not be after you the cowardliest of princes whom flattery would not equate with you, decorating him with your name, with your titles, and with your virtues even'?"

Dialogue de *Sulla and d'Eucrates*

Q<small>UELQUES</small> jours après que Sylla se fut démis de la dictature, j'appris que la réputation que j'avois parmi les philosophes lui faisoit souhaiter de me vois. Il étoit à sa maison de Tibur, où il jouissoit des premiers momens tranquilles de sa vie. Je ne sentis point devant lui le désordre où nous jette ordinairement la présence des grands hommes. Et, dès que nous fûmes seuls: Sylla, lui dis-je, vous vous êtes donc mis vous-même dans cet état de médiocrité qui afflige presque tous les humains? Vous avez renoncé à cet empire que votre gloire & vos vertus vous donnoient sur tous les hommes? La Fortune semble être gênée de ne plus vous élever aux honneurs.

E<small>UCRATE</small>, me dit-il, si je ne suis plus en spectacle à l'univers, c'est la faute des choses humaines, qui ont des bornes, & non pas la mienne. J'ai cru avoir rempli ma destinée, dès que je n'ai plus eu à faire de grandes choses. Je n'étois point fait pour gouverner tranquillement un peuple esclave. J'aime à remporter des victoires, à fonder ou détruire des États, à faire des ligues, à punir un usurpateur: mais, pour ces minces détails de gouvernement où les génies médiocres ont tant d'avantages, cette lente exécution des lois, cette discipline d'une milice tranquille, mon âme ne saurait s'en occuper.

I<small>L EST</small> singulier, lui dis-je, que vous ayez porté tant de délicatesse dans l'ambition. Nous avons bien vu des grands hommes peu touchés du vain éclat & de la pompe qui entourent ceux qui gouvernent: mais il y en a bien peu qui n'aient été sensibles au plaisir de gouverner et de faire rendre, à leur fantaisie, le respect qui n'est dû qu'aux lois.

E<small>T MOI</small>, me dit-il, Eucrate, je n'ai jamais été si peu content, que lorsque je me suis vu maître absolu dans Rome; que j'ai regardé autour de moi, & que je n'ai trouvé ni rivaux ni ennemis.

J'ai cru qu'on diroit quelque jour que je n'avois châtié que des esclaves. Veux-tu, me suis-je dit, que dans ta patrie il n'y ait plus d'hommes qui puissent être touchés de ta gloire? Et, puisque tu établis la tyrannie, ne vois-tu pas bien qu'il n'y aura point après toi de prince si lâche, que la flatterie ne t'égale & ne pare de ton nom, de tes titres & de tes vertus mêmes?

"Seigneur, you are changing all my ideas by the manner in which I see you act. I believed that you had some ambition but no love of glory. I saw well that your soul was elevated, but I did not suspect that it was great. Everything of your life seemed to present to me a man consumed by the desire to rule, and who, full of stormy passions, with pleasure burdened himself with the shame, the reproaches, and the baseness even, which attach to tyranny. Because, finally, you have sacrificed everything to your power, you have made yourself fearful to every Roman; you have exercised without pity the powers of the most terrible magistracy that ever was. The Senate could behold so pitiless a protector only in trembling. Someone said to you, 'Sulla, up to what point will you spill Roman blood? Do you wish to rule only the walls of the city?' It was then that you published those tables which determined the life and the death of every citizen."

"And it is all the blood that I spilled which made it possible for me to perform my greatest deeds. If I had governed the Romans mildly, how wonderful [must that have been]! The boredom, the disgust, a [mere] whim would have made me drop the government! But I resigned the dictatorship, at a point where there was not a single man in the world who could believe other than that the dictatorship was my only shelter. I appeared before the Romans, a citizen amid my fellow-citizens; and I have dared to tell them, I'm ready to give account for all the blood that I've spilled for the Republic. I will answer everyone who will come to question me about father, son, or brother. All the Romans hold their silence before me."

"That lovely action about which you speak to me appears to me most imprudent. It is true that you have had on your side the novel astonishment in which you've placed the Romans. But how did you dare speak to them of justifying yourself, and taking as judges men who owed you so many revenges?

"When all of your deeds would only have been severe for as long as you were master, they became so many frightful crimes from the moment you no longer were so."

"Are you calling crimes," he said to me, "that which has produced the good of the Republic? Should you prefer that I might quietly watch so many senators betray the Senate, or, that people which, imagining that liberty ought to be as complete as slavery can be, sought to abolish the magistracy itself?

SEIGNEUR, vous changez toutes mes idées, de la façon dont je vous vois agir. Je croyois que vous aviez de l'ambition, mais aucun amour pour la gloire je voyois bien que votre âme étoit haute; mais je ne soupçonnais pas qu'elle fût grande: tout, dans votre vie, sembloit me montrer un homme dévoré du désir de commander, & qui, plein des plus funestes passions, se chargeoit, avec plaisir, de la honte, des remords & de la bassesse même attachés à la tyrannie. Car, enfin, vous avez tout sacrifié à votre puissance; vous vous êtes rendu redoutable à tous les Romains; vous avez exercé, sans pitié les fonctions de la plus terrible magistrature qui fût jamais. Le sénat ne vit qu'en tremblant un défenseur si impitoyable. Quelqu'un vous dit: Sylla, jusqu'à quand répandras-tu le sang romain? Veux-tu ne commander qu'à des murailles? Pour lors, vous publiâtes ces tables qui décidèrent de la vie & de la mort de chaque citoyen.

ET C'EST tout le sang que j'ai versé qui m'a mis en état de faire la plus grande de toutes mes actions. Si j'avois gouverné les Romains avec douceur, quelle merveille, que l'ennui, que le dégoût, qu'un caprice m'eussent fait quitter le gouvernement! Mais je me suis démis de la dictature dans le temps qu'il n'y avoit pas un seul homme dans l'univers qui ne crût que la dictature était mon seul asyle. J'ai paru devant les Romains, citoyen au milieu de mes concitoyens; & j'ai osé leur dire: Je suis prêt à rendre compte de tout le sang que j'ai versé pour la République; je répondrai à tous ceux qui viendront me demander leur père, leur fils ou leur frère. Tous les Romains se sont tus devant moi.

Cette belle action dont vous me parlez, me paroît bien imprudente. Il est vrai que vous avez eu pour vous le nouvel étonnement dans lequel vous avez mis les Romains. Mais comment osâtes-vous leur parler de vous justifier, & de prendre pour juges des gens qui vous devaient tant de vengeances?

Quand toutes vos actions n'auroient été que sévères pendant que vous étiez le maître, elles devenoient des crimes affreux dès que vous ne l'étiez plus.

Vous appelez des crimes, me dit-il, ce qui a fait le salut de la République? Vouliez-vous que je visse tranquillement des sénateurs trahir le sénat, pour ce peuple qui, s'imaginant que la liberté doit être aussi extrême que le peut être l'esclavage, cherchoit à abolir la magistrature même?

"The people, hobbled by the laws and by the seriousness of the Senate, have always labored to overthrow both of them. But he who is ambitious enough to serve the people against the Senate and the laws is also ambitious enough to become the people's master. It is thus that we have seen so many republics in Greece and Italy come to an end.

"In order to prevent a similar disaster, the Senate has always been obliged to busy this disobedient crowd in wars. The Senate has been forced in spite of itself to pillage the earth and to subdue so many nations, the obedience of which burdens us. Now that the universe has no more enemies to give us, what could the destiny of the Republic be? And, without me, would the Senate have been able to prevent the people in its blind furor for liberty from delivering itself to Marius or the first tyrant who could have made them hope for independence?

"The gods, who have imparted to most men a lax ambition, have connected nearly as many evils to liberty as to servitude. But whatever the price of that noble liberty must be, it is very necessary to pay it to the gods.

"The sea swallows up vessels and overflows whole countries, and it is nonetheless useful to mankind.

Posterity will decide that which Rome has not yet dared to consider. It will find perhaps that I have not drawn enough blood. Not all the partisans of Marius have been proscribed."

"I must admit it, Sulla, you astonish me. What! It is for the good of your country that you have spilled so much blood? You have had some attachment to your country?"

"Eucrates," he said to me, "I never did have that overpowering love of the country, of which we find so many examples in the first hours of the Republic. And I as much love Coriolanus, who carries the flames and iron right up to the walls of his ungrateful city, who makes every citizen repent of the affront that the citizens offered him, as him that chased the Gauls from the capitol. I have never desired to be the slave, nor the worshipper, of the society of my peers. That love which is so much bandied about is too popular a passion to be compatible with the elevation of my soul. I have only been guided by my reflections and, above all, by the scorn that I've had for men. One may judge, from the manner I've dealt with the only great people in the world, the intensity of my scorn for all others.

Le peuple, gêné par les lois & par la gravité du sénat, a toujours travaillé à renverser l'un & l'autre. Mais celui qui est assez ambitieux pour le servir contre le sénat & les lois, le fut toujours assez pour devenir son maître. C'est ainsi que nous avons vu finir tant de républiques dans la Grèce et dans l'Italie.

Pour prévenir un pareil malheur, le sénat a toujours été obligé d'occuper à la guerre ce peuple indocile. Il a été forcé, malgré lui, à ravager la terre & à soumettre tant de nations dont l'obéissance nous pèse. A présent que l'univers n'a plus d'ennemis à nous donner, quel seroit le destin de la République? Et, sans moi, le sénat auroit-il pu empêcher que le peuple, dans sa fureur aveugle pour la liberté, ne se livrât lui-même à Marius, ou au premier tyran qui lui aurait fait espérer l'indépendance?

Les dieux, qui ont donné à la plupart des hommes une lâche ambition, ont attaché à la liberté presque autant de malheurs qu'à la servitude. Mais, quel que doive être le prix de cette noble liberté, il faut bien le payer aux dieux.

La mer engloutit les vaisseaux, elle submerge des pays entiers; & elle est pourtant utile aux humains.

La postérité jugera ce que Rome n'a pas encore osé examiner: elle trouvera peut-être que je n'ai pas versé assez de sang, & que tous les partisans de Marius n'ont pas été proscrits.

IL FAUT que je l'avoue; Sylla, vous m'étonnez. Quoi! c'est pour le bien de votre patrie que vous avez versé tant de sang? & vous avez eu de l'attachement pour elle?

Eucrate, me dit-il, je n'eus jamais cet amour dominant pour la patrie dont nous trouvons tant d'exemples dans les premiers temps de la République: & j'aime autant Coriolan, qui porte la flamme et le fer jusqu'aux murailles de sa ville ingrate, qui fait repentir chaque citoyen de l'affront que lui a fait chaque citoyen, que celui qui chassa les Gaulois du capitole. Je ne me suis jamais piqué d'être l'esclave ni l'idolâtre de la société de mes pareils: & cet amour tant vanté est une passion trop populaire pour être compatible avec la hauteur de mon âme. Je me suis uniquement conduit-par mes réflexions, & surtout par le mépris que j'ai eu pour les hommes. On peut juger, par la manière dont j'ai traité le seul grand peuple de l'univers, de l'excès de ce mépris pour tous les autres.

"I thought that, being on the earth, it was necessary that I should be free there. Had I been born among barbarians, I would have sought to usurp the throne less for the sake of commanding than for the sake of not being commanded. Born in a republic, I've acquired the glory of a conqueror while seeking only that of free men.

"When I came into Rome with my soldiers, I breathed neither anger nor revenge. I judged without hate, if also without pity, the astonished Romans. 'Were you free,' I said to them, 'and wanted to be slaves? No! Die rather, and you will have the advantage of dying citizens of a free city!'

"I believed that it was the greatest of crimes to overthrow the liberty of a city in which I was a citizen. I have punished that crime, and I haven't been concerned whether I might be the good or the evil genius of the Republic. Meanwhile, the government of our fathers has been restored; the people have paid for all the insults they made to the nobles. Fear has checked the jealousies, and Rome has never been so calm.

"There now, you are instructed about everything that has inclined me towards all the bloody tragedies you have beheld. If I had lived in those happy days of the Republic, where the citizens, tranquil in their homes, offered to the gods a free soul, you would have seen me spend my life in that retirement which, [as it is], I have only obtained by such blood and sweat."

"Seigneur," I told him, "it is happy that heaven should have spared to humankind a number of men such as yourself. Born to mediocrity, we are overburdened by sublime spirits. In order that one man might rise above humanity . . . that costs most dearly to all the rest.

"You have considered the ambition of past heroes as a common passion, and you've only taken seriously that ambition which calculates. The insatiable desire to rule that you have found in the hearts of a few citizens has made you resolve to be an extraordinary man. The love of liberty has made you resolve to be harsh and cruel. Who could say whether a heroism of principle had not been more furious than a heroism of impetuousness? But if, in order to avoid being a slave yourself, it has been necessary for you to usurp dictatorial authority, how have you dared to resign it? The Roman people, you say, have seen you unarmed and have made no attempts against your life. That is a danger from which you've escaped. A greater danger could await you. It could happen that you will one day come to see a great criminal profit from your moderation, and confuse you among the mob of a subjugated people."

J'ai cru qu'étant sur la terre, il falloit que j'y fusse libre. Si j'étois né chez les barbares, j'aurois moins cherché à usurper le trône pour commander, que pour ne pas obéir. Né dans une république, j'ai obtenu la gloire des conquérants, en ne cherchant que celle des hommes libres.

Lorsqu'avec mes soldats je suis entré dans Rome, je ne respirais ni la fureur ni la vengeance. J'ai jugé sans haine, mais aussi sans pitié, les Romains étonnés. Vous étiez libres, ai-je dit, et vous vouliez vivre esclaves? Non. Mais mourez; et vous aurez l'avantage de mourir citoyens d'une ville libre.

J'ai cru qu'ôter la liberté à une ville dont j'étois citoyen, étoit le plus grand des crimes. J'ai puni ce crime-là; et je ne me suis point embarrassé si je serois le bon ou le mauvais génie de la République. Cependant le gouvernement de nos pères a été rétabli; le peuple a expié tous les affronts qu'il avait faits aux nobles: la crainte a suspendu les jalousies; & Rome n'a jamais été si tranquille.

Vous voilà instruit de ce qui m'a déterminé à toutes les sanglantes tragédies que vous avez vues. Si j'avois vécu dans ces jours heureux de la République, où les citoyens, tranquilles dans leurs maisons, y rendoient aux dieux une âme libre, vous m'auriez vu passer ma vie dans cette retraite, que je n'ai obtenue que par tant de sang et de sueur.

Seigneur, lui dis-je, il est heureux que le ciel ait épargné au genre humain le nombre des hommes tels que vous: Nés pour la médiocrité, nous sommes accablés par les esprits sublimes. Pour qu'un homme soit au-dessus de l'humanité, il en coûte trop cher à tous les autres.

Vous avez regardé l'ambition des héros comme une passion commune; et vous n'avez fait cas que de l'ambition qui raisonne. Le désir insatiable de dominer, que vous avez trouvé dans le cœur de quelques citoyens, vous a fait prendre la résolution d'être un homme extraordinaire: l'amour de votre liberté vous a fait prendre celle d'être terrible & cruel. Qui diroit qu'un héroïsme de principe eût été plus funeste qu'un héroïsme d'impétuosité? Mais si, pour vous empêcher d'être esclave, il vous a fallu usurper la dictature, comment avez-vous osé la rendre? Le peuple romain, dites-vous, vous a vu désarmé, & n'a pont attenté sur votre vie. C'est un danger auquel vous avez échappé; un plus grand danger peut vous attendre. Il peut vous arriver de voir quelque jour un grand criminel jouir de votre modération, & vous confondre dans la foule d'un peuple soumis.

"I have a name," he said to me, "and it assures me my safety and that of the Roman people. This name halts every undertaking, and there is no ambition which should not be frightened by it. Sulla breathes, and his genius is more powerful than that of all the Romans. Sulla keeps about him Chaeronea, Orchomenus, and Signion. Sulla has given every Roman family a domestic and harsh example. Every Roman will always have me before his eyes, and, even in his dreams, I will appear before him dripping with blood. He will imagine that he sees the terrible tables and reads his name at the head of those proscribed. They secretly murmur against my laws. But my laws will not be erased even by waves of Roman blood. Am I not in the center of Rome? You will still find at my home the javelin that I held at Orchomenus, and the shield that I carried against the walls of Athens. Am I the less Sulla because I have no lictors [honor guards]? For me I have the Senate, with justice and the laws. The Senate has for itself my genius, my treasure, and my glory."

"I admit," said I to him, "that once make someone tremble, and one maintains almost forever something of the advantage that one gained over him."

"Doubtlessly," he told me. "I have astonished men, and that is a lot. Remember the story of my life: You will see that I have derived everything from this principle, and that it has been the heart of all my deeds. Remind yourself of my disputes with Marius. I was indignant to see a man without a name, proud of the very baseness of his birth, undertake to return the first families of Rome into the mob of the people. In that situation I bore all the weight of a great soul. I was young. I resolved to make myself capable of demanding from Marius an accounting for his insults. For the purpose, I assailed him with his own weapons, that is, triumphs against the enemies of the Republic.

"When at the whim of fate I had to leave Rome, I conducted myself in the same manner. I went to carry war to Mithridates and imagined that I destroyed Marius in order to conquer his enemy. While I left him to profit from his power over the people, I gave him countless mortifications. I forced him every day to journey to the Capitoline to thank the gods for the successes by which I made him desperate. I waged against him a war of reputation crueler by a hundred times than that my legions waged against the barbarian king. Not a single word could he draw from my mouth, which did not indicate my daring. My least deeds, ever superb, were for Marius so many terrible forewarnings. Finally, Mithridates sued for peace. Conditions were favorable, and, if Rome had been quiet,

J'AI un nom, me dit-il; & il me suffit pour ma sûreté & celle du peuple romain. Ce nom arrête toutes les entreprises; & il n'y a point d'ambition qui n'en soit épouvantée. Sylla respire; & son génie est plus puissant que celui de tous les Romains. Sylla a autour de lui Chéronée, Orchomène et Signion; Sylla a donné à chaque famille de Rome un exemple domestique & terrible: chaque Romain m'aura toujours devant les yeux; &, dans ses songes même, je lui apparaîtrai couvert de sang; il croira voir les funestes tables, et lire son nom à la tête des proscrits. On murmure en secret contre mes lois; mais elles ne seront pas effacées par des flots même de sang romain. Ne suis-je pas au milieu de Rome? Vous trouverez encore chez moi le javelot que j'avois à Orchomène, et le bouclier que je portai sur les murailles d'Athènes. Parce que je n'ai point de licteurs, en suis-je moins Sylla? J'ai pour moi le sénat, avec la justice et les lois; le sénat a pour lui mon génie, ma fortune & ma gloire.

J'AVOUE, le dis-je, que, quand on a une fois fait trembler quelqu'un, on conserve presque toujours quelque chose de l'avantage qu'on a pris.

SANS doute, me dit-il. J'ai étonné les hommes, & c'est beaucoup. Repassez dans votre mémoire l'histoire de ma vie: vous verrez que j'ai tout tiré de ce principe, et qu'il a été l'âme de toutes mes actions. Ressouvenez-vous de mes démêlés avec Marius: je fus indigné de voir un homme sans nom, fier de la bassesse de sa naissance, entreprendre de ramener les premières familles de Rome dans la foule du peuple; &, dans cette situation, je portais tout le poids d'une grande âme. J'étois jeune, et je résolus de me mettre en état de demander compte à Marius de ses mépris. Pour cela, je l'attaquai avec ses propres armes, c'est-à-dire par des victoires contre les ennemis de la République.

Lorsque, par le caprice du sort, je fus obligé de sortir de Rome, je me conduisis de même: j'allai faire la guerre à Mithridate; & je crus détruire Marius, à force de vaincre l'ennemi de Marius. Pendant que je laissois ce Romain jouir de son pouvoir sur la populace, je multiplois ses mortifications; & je le forçois tous les jours d'aller au capitole rendre grâces aux dieux des succès dont je le désespérois. Je lui faisois une guerre de réputation, plus cruelle cent fois que celle que mes légions faisoient au roi barbare. Il ne sortoit pas un seul mot de ma bouche, qui ne marquât mon audace; & mes moindres actions, toujours superbes, étoient pour Marius de funestes présages. Enfin Mithridate demanda la paix; les conditions étoient raisonnables: &, si Rome avoit été tranquille,

or if my fortune had not been touch and go, I would have accepted them. But the poor condition of my affairs forced me to make them more severe. I insisted that he would destroy his fleet and that he would return to his neighboring kings all the states of which he had deprived them. 'I leave to you,' I told him, 'the kingdom of your forefathers, to you who ought to thank me that I would leave you the very hand with which you signed the decree to kill in a single day a hundred thousand Romans.' Mithridates remained motionless and Marius, at the center of Rome, trembled at it.

"That same daring, which served me so well against Mithridates, against Marius, against his son, against Telesinus, and against the people—which has sustained my entire dictatorship—has also protected my life in the day that I abandoned the dictatorship. That day assures my liberty forever."

"Seigneur," I said to him, "Marius reasoned just as you do when, covered with the blood of his enemies and that of Romans, he showed that audacity which you have punished. You have indeed for yourself a few more triumphs and a few more excesses. But, in taking the dictatorship, you have given an example of the very crime that you punished. There is the example which will be followed and not that of a moderation that folk will only admire.

"Once the gods had suffered Sulla in all impunity to make himself dictator of Rome, they thence banished liberty for ever. They would have to make far too many miracles now, in order to strip the heart of every Roman captain of the ambition to reign. You have taught them that there was a very much surer path to acquire tyranny and keep it without peril. You have divulged that fatal secret and unveiled that which alone made the good citizens of a republic too rich and too great: no hope of the power to oppress it."

His visage changed and he was quiet for a moment. "I fear," he said to me with emotion, "only one man in whom I think I behold several Mariuses. Chance, or perhaps a stronger destiny, caused me to spare him. I watch him ceaselessly. I study his soul, for there he hides some proud designs. But if ever he forms the intention to rule over men whom I have made my equals, I swear by the gods that I will punish his insolence."

End of the Dialogue of Sulla and Eucrates

ou si ma fortune n'avoit pas été chancelante, je les aurois acceptées. Mais le mauvais état de mes affaires m'obligea de les rendre plus dures; j'exigeai qu'il détruisît sa flotte, & qu'il rendît aux rois ses voisins tous les états dont il les avait dépouillés. Je te laisse, lui dis-je, le royaume de tes pères, à toi qui devrois me remercier de ce que je te laisse la main avec laquelle tu as signé l'ordre de faire mourir en un jour cent mille Romains. Mithridate resta immobile; & Marius, au milieu de Rome, en trembla.

Cette même audace, qui m'a si bien servi contre Mithridate, contre Marius, contre son fils, contre Thélésinus, contre le peuple, qui a soutenu toute ma dictature, a aussi défendu ma vie le jour que je l'ai quittée: et ce jour assure ma liberté pour jamais.

Seigneur, lui dis-je, Marius raisonnoit comme vous, lorsque, couvert du sang de ses ennemis & de celui des Romains, il montroit cette audace que vous avez punie. Vous avez bien pour vous quelques victoires de plus; & de plus grands excès. Mais, en prenant la dictature, vous avez donné l'exemple du crime que vous avez puni. Voilà l'exemple qui sera suivi, & non pas celui d'une modération qu'on ne fera qu'admirer.

Quand les dieux ont souffert que Sylla se soit impunément fait dictateur dans Rome, ils y ont proscrit la liberté pour jamais. Il faudroit qu'ils fissent trop de miracles, pour arracher à présent du cœur de tous les capitaines romains l'ambition de régner. Vous leur avez appris qu'il y avoit une voie bien plus sûre pour aller à la tyrannie, & la garder sans péril. Vous avez divulgué ce fatal secret, & ôté ce qui fait seul les bons citoyens d'une république trop riche et trop grande: le désespoir de pouvoir l'opprimer.

Il changea de visage, & se tut un moment. Je ne crains, me dit-il avec émotion, qu'un homme dans lequel je crois voir plusieurs Marius. Le hasard, ou bien un destin plus fort, me l'a fait épargner. Je le regarde sans cesse; j'étudie son âme: il y cache des desseins profonds. Mais, s'il ose jamais former celui de commander à des hommes que j'ai faits mes égaux, je jure par les dieux que je punirai son insolence.

Fin du dialogue de Sylla et d'Eucrate

Commentary

Translated excerpts follow, in the form of a character portrait from *The Spirit of the Laws* (A) and a political analysis from *Considerations on the Greatness of the Romans and their Decline* (B).

A.

Sulla, who confused tyranny, anarchy, and liberty, passed the Cornelian laws. He seemed to make regulations only for the sake of creating crimes. Thus, characterizing an infinity of actions with the name murder, he discovered murderers everywhere. By a practice which was only too much followed, he held out traps, sowed thorns, and opened abyssess in the paths of all the citizens.

Nearly all of Sulla's laws bore only the interdiction of water and fire. Caesar added the confiscation of property to them.[4] For the rich, holding their patrimony in exile, were more emboldened to commit crimes.

The emperors having established a military government, they soon felt that it was no less harsh against themselves than against the subjects. They sought to moderate it. They believed that they needed some dignities and the respect one would have for them.

They approached monarchy somewhat, and they divided penalties into three classes:[5] the ones which affected the principal persons of the state,[6] and which were gentle enough; the ones which they inflicted on persons of an inferior rank,[7] and which were more severe; finally, the ones which only touched the base classes,[8] and which were the most rigorous. (VI, 15)

When Sulla wished to restore Rome's liberty, she was no longer able to receive it. She possessed no more than the feeble remains of virtue, and inasmuch as she always had less of it afterwards, instead of rousing herself after Caesar, Tiberius, Gaius, Claudius, Nero, and Domitian, she was always further enslaved. Every blow fell upon the tyrants, none upon the tyranny. (III, 3)

One notes, in the wars of Marius and Sulla, the extent to which souls, among the Romans were little by little corrupted. Such fatal things caused it to be imagined that one would see them no more. But, under the *triumviri*, they wanted to be more cruel, while appearing less. It is distressing to behold the sophisms that cruelty made use of. One finds in Appian (d)[9] the formula for proscriptions. You would say that they had no objective in this but the good of the republic, as they speak with so much cold blood, show so many advantages, so much are the means that they adopt preferable to others, so far will the wealthy be safe, so far will the vulgar be tranquil, so much do they fear to place the citizens' lives in danger, so much do they wish to appease the soldiers, and, finally, how very happy everyone will be. (XII, 18)

B.

The soldiers therefore began to acknowledge only their general, founding all their hopes in him and seeing the city from greater distance. They were no longer the solidiers of the Republic but of Sulla, Marius, Pompey, Caesar. Rome was no longer able to to know whether he who was at the head of an army in a province was its general or its enemy. (*Romains*, IX, p.412)

I pray that one might allow me to deflect attention from the horrors of the wars of Marius and Sulla: one will find the frightening history in Appian. Over and above the jealousy, the ambition, and the curelty of the two leaders, each Roman was furious; new and old citizens no longer considered themselves as members of the same republic,[10] and they waged a war of a particular character that was at once civil and foreign.

Sulla made certain laws most fit for removing the cause of the disorders that they beheld: he enhanced the authority of the Senate, balanced the power of the people, regulated that of the tribunes. The fancy that caused him to quit the dictatorship seemed to give life to the Republic; but, in the furor of his successes, he had done things that placed Rome in an impossible situation for recovering its liberty.

He ruined all military discipline through his Asian campaign: he habituated his army to rapine,[11] and he gave it needs that it had never had. Once he corrupted the soldiers, that had in the end to corrupt the captains.

He entered Rome arms in hand and instructed Roman generals to violate liberty's asylum.[12]

He gave the citizen's properties to the soldiers,[13] and he made them forever greedy: for, from that very moment, there were no longer any warriors who did not anticipate an opportunity that would place their fellow-citizens goods into their hands.

He invented proscriptions and placed a price upon the head of all those who were not of his faction. Thereafter, it was impossible further to commit oneself to the Republic; for, between two ambitious men, and who were rivals for victory, those who were neutral and partisans of liberty were certain to be proscribed by whoever of the two would be victorious. It were therefore prudent to commit oneself to one of the two.

There came after him (Sulla), Cicero said,[14] a man who, in an impious cause and a still more shameful victory, did not only confiscate the property of individuals but swept up entire provinces in the same calamity.

Sulla, abandoning the dictatorship, had seemed to want to live only under the protection of his own laws. But that deed, which signaled such great moderation, was itself a consequence of his violence acts. He had awarded establishments to forty-seven legions in differing places around Italy. Those men, Appian said, considering their fortunes as connected with his life, watched over his safety and were always ready to aid or avenge him.[15]

The Republic being destined to perish, there was no longer any question but to know how and by whom it had to be felled.

Two equally ambitious men, save that one of them did not know how to pursue his goal so directly as the other, eclipsed by their credits, by their exploits, by their virtues all the other citizens: Pompey appreared the foremost and Caesar followed very closely.

Pompey, in order to attact favor, caused Sulla's laws which limited the power of the people to be overturned, and, when he had made his country's most salutary laws a sacrifice to his ambition, he obtained everything that he wanted, and the people's audacity in regard to him was unlimited.

Rome's laws had wisely distributed public authority to a large number of magistracies, which supported, checked, and balanced one another; and, insofar as they all had only a limited power, each citizen was fit for attaining it, and the people, seeing many personalities one after another pass before them, became fixed on none of them. But, in those times, the Republic's system changed: the most powerful made the people give them exceptional commissions, which annihilated the authority of the people and the magistrates and placed every great matter into the hands of one alone or very few folk.[16]

Was it necessary to wage war against Sertorius? They gave the commission to Pompey. Was it necessary to wage war against Mithridates? Everybody shouted out: "Pompey." Had people a need to bring wheat to Rome? The people believed they would be lost if they did not hand the charge of it to Pompey. Does one want to destroy the pirates? Only

Pompey is fit for it. And, when Caesar threatened to invade, the Senate in its turn cried for and placed hope in none but Pompey.

"I indeed believe," said Marcus to the people,[17] "that Pompey, whom the nobles wait for, would much prefer assuring your liberty than their domination; but there was a time when each of you had the protection of many, and not all the protection of a single man, and when it was unheard of that a mortal could give or take away such things."

In Rome, designed to aggrandize itself, it had been necessary to concentrate in the same persons honors and authority; the which in times of trouble could collect the management of the people in a single citizen.

When folk grant honors, they know precisely what they give; but when they connect it with power, they cannot to say to what length it will be able to be borne.

Excessive privileges accorded to one citizen in a republic always have some necessary consequences: they cause the people's envy to generate, or they augment their love beyond limits.

Twice returning to Rome, a master to oppress the Republic, Pompey had the moderation to dismiss his armies before entering the city, and to appear in it as a simple citizen. Those actions, which covered him with glory, caused that, subsequently, whatever thing that he might have done to the prejudice of the laws, the Senate declared itself on his behalf.

Pompey had an ambition slower and gentler than that of Ceasear: the latter wished to attain sovereign authority arms in hand, like Sulla. That fashion of oppressing displeased Pompey: he aspired to the dictatorship, but by means of the people's suffrage; he could not agree to usurp authority, but he would have wished that folk had confided it into his hands.

Since the people's favor is never constant, there were some times when Pompey saw his credit diminishing;[18] and, the thing that affected him most sensibly, some men whom he scorned increased their credit and used it against him.

That caused him to do three equally fatal things: he corrupted the people by means of money and inserted into the elections a price on the suffrages of each citizen.

Moreover, he made use of the vilest population in order to disturb the magistrates in their functions, hoping that the wise men, fatigued with living in anarchy, would create him dictator from desperation.

Finally, he connected his interests with Caesar and Crassus. Cato said that it was not their antagonism that lost the Republic, but their union. Effectively, Rome was in that unhappy condition that it was less burdened by the civil wars than by the peace, which, concentrating the views and the interests of the principal persons, made nothing more than a tyranny.

Pompey did not intend to lend his credit to Caesar, but, without knowing it, he sacrificed it to him. Soon Ceasar used against him the forces that he had entrusted to Ceasar, and even his stratagems; he disturbed the city by his emissaries and made himself master of the elections: consuls, praetors, tribunes were purchased at the prices that they themselves set.

The Senate, which clearly saw Caesar's designs, had recourse to Pompey: he begged them to take up the defense of the Republic, if one could call by that name a government which required protection from one of its citizens.

I believe that what above all destroyed Pompey was the shame that he had for thinking that by elevating Caesar, as he had done, he might have failed in foresight. He embraced that idea as late as he could; he did not set himself up in defense, in order not to admit that he had placed himself in danger; he maintained, in the Senate, that Caesar would not dare to wage war, and, because he had said it so often, he always repeated it.

It seemed that one thing placed Caesar in condition to undertake all; that is that, by an unfortunate similarity of names, they had connected his government of Cisalpine Gaul with that of Gaul beyond the Alps.

Politics did not allow that armies should be round about Rome; but neither did it tolerate that Italy would be altogether disfurnished of troops. That caused that they kept considerable forces in Cisalpine Gaul, which is to say in the land that is from the Rubicon, a small river in Romagna, up to the Alps. But in order to protect the city of Rome from these troops, they made the famous senatus-consultum that folk still see engraved on the highway from Rimini to Cesena, by which they dedicated to the infernal gods, and declared a sacrilege and parricide anyone who with a legion, with an army or with a cohort would pass the Rubicon.

To such a large government, which kept the town in check, they attached another that was greater still: that was the one of Transalpine Gaul, which comprised the lands from the south of France; which, having given Caesar for several years the occasion to wage war against all the peoples he wanted, caused his soldiers to age with him, and that he conquered them no less than the barbarians. If Caesar had not held the government of Transalpine Gaul, he could not have corrupted his soliders, nor caused such renown for his name by so many victories. If he had not had that of Cisalpine Gaul, Pompey would have been able to stop him at the passage of the Alps; instead, from the beginning of the war, he was forced to quit Italy; which caused his faction to lose reputation, which, in civil wars, is authority itself.

The same fright that Hannibal carried into Rome after the battle of Cannes, Caesar there spread when he passed the Rubicon. Pompey, distracted, saw in the first moments of the war no part to take but that which befalls matters of desperation: he knew nothing but to yield and to flee; he fled Rome, leaving there the public treasury; he could nowhere impede the conqueror; he abandoned a part of his troops, all of Italy and went beyond the sea.

Folk speak much of Caesar's luck. But that extraordinary man had so many great qualities, without one defect, although he had many vices, that it had been most difficult if, whatever army he had commanded, it would not have been victorious, and if in any republic that he been born he had not governed it.

Caesar, after having defeated Pompey's lieutenants in Spain, went into Greece to look for him. Pompey, who held the sea coast and superior forces, was on the point of seeing Caesar's army destroyed by misery and hunger. But, as he had overwhelmingly the weakness of wanting to be approved, he could not prevent himself from lending an ear to the vain discourses of his people, who ceaselessly encouraged or accused him.[19] "He wishes," said one, "to perpetuate himself in command and be, like Agamemnon, the king of kings."—"I warn you," another said, "that we will not again eat the figs of Tusculum this year." Whatever particular successes he had managed to turn the heads of that senatorial troop. Thus, in order not to be blamed, he did one thing that posterity will blame forever, by sacrificing so many advantages in order to proceed with new troops to combat an army that so often conquered.

When the remnant from Pharsalia had withdrawn into Africa, Scipio, who commanded them, never wanted to follow Cato's advice, to draw out the war at length: boosted by some advantages, he risked everything and lost everything; and, when Brutus and Cassius re-established that faction, the same precipitate action lost the Republic a third time.[20]

You will observe that, in the civil wars that lasted such a long time, the authority of Rome ceaselessly increased externally: under Marius,

Sulla, Pompey, Caesar, Antony, Augustus, Rome, always more terrifying, succeeded in destroying all the kings that yet remained.

There is no state that so strongly threatens others with conquest than the one that is in the horrors of a civil war: everyone, noble, bourgeois, craftsman, laborer, becomes a soldier; and, whenever, by peace, the forces are reunited, that state has such great advantages over the others, which hardly have anything but some citizens. Besides, in civil wars, great men often arise, because, in the confusion, those who have any merit break out, each seeks and establishes himself at his rank; whereas, in other times, folk are assigned and they are almost always out of place. And, in order to pass on from the Roman examples to others more recent, the French have never been so fearful externally as following the quarrels of the houses of Burgundy and Orléans, following the troubles of the Augsburg League, following the civil wars during the miniority of Louis XIII and that of Louis XIV.[21] England has never been so respected as under Cromwell, after the wars of the Long Parliament. The Germans have gained superiority over the Turks only after the German civil wars. The Spanish, under Phillippe V, initially after the civil wars of the Succession, manifested in Sicily a force that has astonished Europe. And today we see Persia from the ashes of civl war regenerating and humiliating the Turks.

Finally, the Republic was oppressed, and it is not necessary to blame the ambition of particular individuals; it is necessary to blame man, always more avid for power to the extent that he has more of it, and who desires all only because he possesses much.

If Caesar and Pompey had thought like Cato, others would have thought as Caesar and Pompey did, and the Republic, destined to perish, would have been dragged to the precipice by another hand.

Caesar pardonned everyone. But it seems to me that the moderation that one manifests after one has usurped everything does not merit great praise.

Whatever one might say about his diligence after Pharsalia, Cicero blames him for delay with reason: he said to Cassius that he would never have believed that Pompey's faction would have thus retreated to Spain and Africa, and that, if they had been able to foresee that Caesar would have busied himself with his war at Alexandria, they would never have made their peace, and they would have withdrawn with Scipio and Cato in Africa.[22] Therefore a foolish love caused him to encounter four wars, and by not forestalling the two last, he rendered doubtful what had been determined at Pharsalia.

Caesar at first governed under the titles of magistracy; for men are hardly only affected by anything but names. And, inasmuch as the peoples of Asia abhorred those of consul and of proconsul, the European peoples detested that of king; in such manner that, in those times, those names caused happiness or despair throughout the earth. Caesar did permit attempting to place the crown on his head; but, seeing that the people stopped their applause, he rejected it. He made still other attempts,[23] and I cannot understand how he might have believed that the Romans, in order to suffer the tyrant, would have loved the tyranny or would have imagined that they did what they had done.

One day the Senate conferred certain honors upon him. He neglected to rise, and, on that occasion, the gravest of the bodies reached the end of patience.

One never offends men so much as when one shocks their ceremonies and their habitual practices. Seek to oppress them; that is sometimes a proof of the esteem you hold for them. Shock their customs; that is always a sign of scorn.

Caesar, forever an enemy to the Senate, could not disguise the scorn that he conceived for that body, which had become nearly ridiculous since it no longer had any authority. For that reason, even his clemency was insulting. Folk noticed that he did not pardon, but that he disdained to punish.

He carried scorn to the point of naming senatus-consulta himself: he enrolled them under the name of the first senators that came into his mind. "I sometimes learn," said Cicero,[24] "that a senatus-consultum passed on my proposal has been borne into Syria and into Armenia before I might have known that it had been made, and several princes have written me letters of thanks because I had proposed that they be would be given the title of king, whom I not only did not know to be kings but even that they might exist in the world."

One can observe in the letters of some great men from those times[25] (that have been assigned the name of Cicero because most of them are by him) the depression and despair of the leading men of the Republic at that sudden revolution, which deprived them of all their honors and even their occupations, when, the Senate being without functions, the credit that they had had throughout the earth, they could no longer hope to have apart from the chamber of a single man. And that is indeed better observed in those letters than in the discourses of historians: they are the masterpiece of the naiveté of folk united by a common sadness and from a century in which false politeness had not everywhere disseminated falsehood; in sum, one does not there see some folk who want to deceive themselves, as in most of our modern letters, but some unhappy friends who seek to declare all.

It was indeed a hard thing, that Caesar should not be able to defend his life; most of the conspirators were from his faction or had been showered by him with benefactions.[26] And the reason for this is most natural: they had found such great advantages in his victory; but the more their fortune became better, the more they began to share in the common misfortune,[27] for, to a man that has nothing, it matters very little, in some regards, what becomes of the government under which he lives.

Further, there was a certain law of nations, an established opinion in all the republics of Greece and Italy, which caused the assassin of him that had usurped sovereign authority to be considered as a virtuous man. In Rome, above all, since the expulsion of the kings, the law was precise, the examples received: the Republic armed the hands of every citizen, making him magistrate for the moment, and dedicated him to her defense.

Brutus indeed dares to say to his friends that, when his father would return to the earth, he would kill him in the same way;[28] and, although from the continuation of the tyranny that spirit of liberty gradually declined, the conspiracies, in the commencement of Augustus's reign, always revived.

That was a dominant love of the fatherland which, deriving from ordinary rules for crimes and virtues, listened only to it and saw neither citizen, nor friend, nor benefactor, nor father: virtue seemed to forget itself in order to exceed itself, and, it caused to be wondered at as divine the action that one at first glance would not approve because it was atrocious.

In effect, was not the crime of Caesar, who lived under a free government, very far beyond being punished other than by assassination? And to inquire why folk had not prosecuted him with open force or by the laws, is not that to seek reasons for his crimes? (*Romains*, XI, pp. 419-431)

That frightful tyranny of the emperors came from the general spirit of the Romans. Inasmuch as they fell at at once under an arbitrary government, and since there was virtually not among them any interval between commanding and serving, they were not prepared for this transition by gentle morals; the ferocious humor remained; the citizens were treated like they had themselves treated conquered enemies, and were governed on the same plan. Sulla entering Rome was not a different man than Sulla entering Athens: he enforced the same law of nations. For states that have not been imperceptibly subjected, when laws fail them, they are still governed by morals. (*Romains*, XV)

It has been called into question whether Augustus had truly had the intention to renounce the empire. But who does not see that, if he had wanted [to do] it, it was impossible that he could succeed at it? Which shows that it was a game, that he demanded every ten years that they might relieve him of that weight, and that he carried always. Those were petty finesses to attract still to himself what he did not imagine sufficiently to have acuired. I reason from the whole of Augustus's life, and, though men are quite bizarre, nevertheless it happens most rarely that they renounce in a moment what they have pursued during their whole life. All Augustus's actions, all his regulations, visibly inclined to the establishment of monarchy. Sulla renounced the dictatorship; but, in all the life of Sulla, amidst his violent exploits, one observes a republican spirit: all his regulations, though tyrannically executed, always inclined to a certain form of republic. Sulla, a driven man, violently led the Romans to liberty. Augustus, a scheming tyrant,[29] gently led them to servitude. While, under Sulla, the Republic regained its strength, everybody cried out "tyranny;" and while, under Augustus, the tyranny strengthened, folk spoke only of liberty.

The custom of triumphs, which had contributed so much to Rome's greatness, was lost under Augustus, or rather that honor became a privilege of sovereignty.[30] Most of the things that occurred under the emperors had their origin in the Republic,[31] and it is necessary to compare them; the latter alone had a right to demand the triumph under the auspices by which the war was conducted:[32] Now it is always conducted under the auspicies of the leader and, consequently by the emperor, who was the leader of every army. (*Romains*, XIII, pp. 441-42)

Claudius managed to destroy the ancient ranks by giving the right of rendering justice to his officers.[33] The wars of Marius and Sulla were mainly waged only to know who would possess this right, the senators or the knights.[34] The whim of an imbecile took it away from the one and the other: a strange outcome of a dispute that had set the whole universe aflame!

There is no authority more absolute than that of the prince that succeeds to a republic: for he finds himself holding all the authority of the
people that had not been able to limit itself.

The unfortunate custom of proscription Sulla introduced continued
under the emperors, and it were indeed required that a prince would
have some virtue in order not to follow it; for, since his ministers and his
favorites aimed at first at so great confiscations, they spoke to him only
of the need to punish and the dangers of clemency. (*Romains*, XVI, p.
462)

Sulla and Sertorius, in the fury of the civil wars, preferred perishing
to doing something from which Mithridates could draw advantage. But,
in the times that followed, as soon as a minister or some grandee believed that it mattered for his greed, for his vengeance, for his ambition,
to cause the barbarians to come into the empire, he at once gave it to
them to ravage.[35] (*Romains*, XVIII, 485)

Conclusion

Now we entertain the paradox, that Montesquieu the historian/philoso-
pher has provided the commentary upon the fictional work of Montesquieu
the poet. The first observation to make in that regard is that the poet says
the same thing about the subject, Sulla, that the historian/philosopher
says about the same subject. Apparently, the poem is less a work of
fiction than it presents to be.

However, there is a further consideration that decisively affects our
commentary, and points to the ultimate significance of this particular
fable. While Montesquieu the poet agrees with the Montesquieu the his-
torian/philosopher concerning the historical figure, Sulla, Sulla's interlocutor, Eucrates, is altogether fictional. Eucrates does not appear in the
work of Montesquieu the historian/philosopher. The lone qualification
of that observation is that the historian/philosopher, as author, is indeed
present in the historical narration. But the fictional philosopher presents
a view of the philosopher's judgment of Sulla that is able to be expressed
directly to Sulla, rather than as the indirect and necessarily abstract interpretation by the narrative historian. In other words, the purpose of the
dialogue *Sulla and Eucrates* is to amplify the voice of the philosopher in
conversation with the tyrant. Moreover, since it was crafted subsequently
to the *Lysimachus*, the conversation there presumably goes beyond the

discussion of "counsel" that characterized the relation of the philosopher and the tyrant in the prior fable.

But what is there beyond the discourse concerning counsel, that makes dramatic representation of the tyrant and the philosopher intellectually significant beyond what the philosopher might say of the tyrant in a narrative history? Where it sufficed for Lysimachus, informed by the philosopher's smiles, to declare, "my people are happy, and so am I," for Sulla, whose happiness derives from private meditations, the question of what would come after him is more important than present joys in the assessment of political happiness. There is, in other words, a disjunct between his happiness and his people's happiness.

The narrative history identifed Sulla as "a republican spirit: all his regulations, though tyrannically executed, always inclined to a certain form of republic." Eucrates, however, testifies to having believed him a man moved by ambition alone and having learned only from conversation that he had a true "love of glory." In short, the philosopher uncovered in the soul of the tyrant a kinship with his own soul. The tyrant is not moved by "that love which is so much bandied about" and which is not "compatible with the elevation of my soul." Because the eros of the tyrant is not the petty eros of the mediocre many, the tyrant "guided by my reflections" holds the same view that Eucrates announced when he described the "mediocrity which afflicts nearly all humans."

Sulla responded to Eucrates by identifying the limits of the "human things" as making it impossible for ordinary men to appreciate the dimensions of his soul—dimensions that render the "petty details" of government that give the advantage to "mediocre minds" unattractive to his great soul. Eucrates found it singular that Sulla was not "sensitive to the pleasure of governing" and commanding in his person the "respect which is due only to the laws." That means, however, that he discovered that the tyrant looked upon the human things from the same eminence the philosopher affects. Their minds are as one in that regard. The mind of the philosopher-king is the place where the tyrant and the philosopher become one.

Although Sulla is prepared to be accountable for all his deeds—as evidenced by his seeking out Eucrates for conversation—Eucrates's new understanding of Sulla's soul ("you are changing all my ideas") does not deflect his judgment about the political meaning of Sulla's rule. The deeds Sulla is prepared to justify even before the mediocre men he now makes his fellow-citizens are only "so many frightful crimes" once Sulla is just another citizen. Sulla responds, in effect, that none can call crimes what "produced the good of the Republic." That is, his justification before his fellow citizens would be that what he did was necessary to sustain their liberty. Sulla knows, however, that he sustained their liberty not against foreign enemies so much as against their own improvidence. Accordingly, his justification depends upon demonstrating to men that they are not capable of understanding and preferring their own good (men of "lax ambition"), and they must be content to allow "posterity" to judge whether they benefited from decent rule.

Eucrates challenged the apparent notion that Sulla acted on the basis of a hyper patriotism, but Sulla quickly disabused him of any such notion, indicating that he took command mainly in order to avoid being ruled by worse men. That motivation to rule is none other than the motive Socrates urges upon the best men—ultimately the philosopher king. Sulla's claim, therefore, is that he has done what Eucrates—the good ruler—would have been required to do upon philosophical grounds. Because the historian-philosopher in his narrative history had already confirmed Sulla's patriotism, Eucrates's "discovery" can only suggest that the philosopher insists upon a justification for such conduct over and above the justification Sulla was prepared to provide for his countrymen.

Eucrates confirms that reading, once Sulla asserts that he has fully instructed Eucrates, by observing that it is a heavenly blessing that men such as himself have been few in the world. For, he insists, "born to mediocrity, we are overbudened by sublime spirits." Does Eucrates mean to argue, therefore, that there is no basis for the rule of philosopher kings? His initial reflection holds that a Sulla who has stepped down has opened the door to the very abuse he sought to cure, the prospect of being governed by worse men: "you will one day come to see a great criminal profit from your moderation, and confuse you among the mob of subjugated people." Sulla, however, retorts that argument with the power of the example that he set, and its enduring sway over the opinions of the people. His "name," he held, assures his safety. When Eucrates conceded the powerful influence of a great example, Sulla went on to recount his battles and his deeds and the manner in which they shaped expectation. Eucrates, though, suggests a further weakness in the argument, namely, that the example of his tyranny will move, not the people at large, but some other great soul, while the example of his moderation will win only general admiration (of the sort the narrative history recounts).

Eucrates, reaching the peak of his argument, insists that far from saving Rome's liberty, Sulla actually "banished liberty for ever." "You have divulged the fatal secret and unveiled that which alone made the good citizens of a republic too rich and too great: no hope of the power to oppress it."

Here Sulla paused. He confessed a fear in this regard. There was one soul that escaped Sulla's revenges and that might pose just such a danger that could not be averted. Sulla, however, says that even from his status as a private citizen, he will keep his eye on that soul and that if he ever begins to pose a threat to men Sulla has made Sulla's equals, "I swear by the gods that I will punish his insolence."

It is good that Sulla swore by the gods in taking aim at Caesar, whom the narrative history shows did exactly as Eucrates "foretold." In swearing by the gods, in these the last words of the dialogue, he allowed the philosopher silently to reclaim his pre-eminence in relation to the tyrant. Inasmuch as tyrant and philosopher are two sides of a single soul, they are distinguished only by what the philosopher learns, namely, how to die. For swearing by the gods is tantamount to expressing the conditional prayer, "if I should live." The tyrant acted as if he did not exist under the bar of death. The philosopher, by contrast, learns first of all the necessity that is death. It is politics that endures—not rulers, politics, the domain of the mediocre.

Notes

1. Debra Nails, *The People of Plato: A Prosopography of Plato and Other Socratics*. Indianapolis: Hackett, 2002.

2. Cf. notes 17-19, chap. 2 above.

3. Sulla was Lucius Corneliuis, who lived from 138–78 BCE. He concluded his victory at Athens in 85 BCE, and returned to Italy by 83 BCE and was master of Rome by 82 BCE. While he did wage political battle against Marius's political party (he had notably opposed them in the "social war"), Marius actually died in late 86BCE, shortly after establishing his dictatorship, and before Sulla had actually returned. When Sulla established his dictatorship, he scattered Marius's ashes in the Anio.

4. Pœnas facinorum auxit, cùm locupletes eo facilius scelere se obligarent, quod integris patrimoniis exularent. Suétone, in Julio Caesare. (Original note)

5. Voyez la loi 3, § [5] *legis ad legem* Cornel *de sicariis*, et un très grand nombre d'autres, au Digeste et au Code. (Original note)

6. Sublimiores. (Original note)

7. Medios. (Original note)

8. Infimos. Leg. 3, § [5] legis ad leg. Cornel. de sicariis. (Original note)

9. *Des guerres civiles*, liv. IV [2, 1]. (Original note)

10. Comme Marius, pour se faire donner la commission de la guerre contre Mithridate au préjudice de Sylla, avait, par le secours du tribun Sulpitius, répandu les huit nouvelles tribus des peuples d'Italie dans les anciennes, ce qui rendait les Italiens maîtres des suffrages, ils étaient la plupart du parti de Marius, pendant que le sénat et les anciens citoyens étaient du parti de Sylla. (Original note)

11. Voyez, dans la *Conjuration de Catilina*, le portrait que Salluste nous fait de cette armée. (Original note)

12. *Fugatis Marii copiis, primus urbem Romam cum armis ingressus est.* (Fragment de Jean d'Antioche, dans l'*Extrait des vertus et des vices.* (Original note)

13. On distribua bien au commencement une partie des terres des ennemis vaincus: mais Sylla donnait les terres des citoyens. (Original note)

14. *Offices*, livre II, chapitre VIII, [M].—*Secutus est, qui in causa impia, victoria etiam fœdiore, non singulorum civium bona publicaret, sed universas provincias regionesque uno calamitatis jure comprehenderet.* (Original note)

15. On peut voir ce qui arriva après la mort de César. (Original note)

16. *Plebis opes immunitæ, paucorum potentia crevit.* (Salluste, *de Conjurat. Catil.* (Original note)

17. Fragment de l'*Histoire de Salluste.—Mihi quidem satis spectatum est, Pompeium tantæ gloriæ adolescentem malle principem volentibus vobis esse, quam illis dominationis socium: auctoremque in primis fore tribunitiæ potestatis. Verum, quirites, antea singuli cives in pluribus, non in uno cuncti præsidia habebatis: neque mortalium quisquam dare aut eripere talia unus poterat.* Le livre III de ces fragments renferme le discours de Marcus Lépidus, tribun du peuple. (Original note)

18. Voyez Plutarque. (Original note)

19. Voyez Plutarque, *Vie de Pompée*. (Original note)

20. Cela est bien expliqué dans Appien, *de la Guerre civile*, livre IV. L'armée d'Octave et d'Antoine aurait péri de faim si l'on n'avait pas donné la bataille. (Original note)

21. Ligue d'Augsbourg. "Ligue qui a donné son nom à la coalition des puissances européennes contre la France, de 1686 à 1697" *(Lar. encyclop.).* [Tresor] (Original note)

22. *Épîtres familières*, livre XV. (Original note)

23. Il cassa les tribuns du peuple. (Original note)

24. *Lettres familières*, liv. IX.—*Ante audio senatusconsultum in Armeniam et Syriam esse perlatum, quod in meam sententiam factum esse dicatur, quam omnino mentionem ullam de ea re esse factam. Atque nolim me jocari putes. Nam mihi scito jam a regibus ultimis allatas esse litteras, quibus mihi gratias agant, quod se mea sententia reges appellaverim: quos ego non modo reges appellatos, sed omnino natos nesciebam.* (Epist. XV.) (Original note)

25. Voyez les lettres de Cicéron et de Sulpitius. (Original note)

26. Décimus Brutus, Caius Casca, Trébonius, Tullius Cimber, Minutius Basillus, étaient amis de César. (Appien, *de Bello civili*, lib. II. (Original note)

27. Je ne parle pas des satellites d'un tyran, qui seraient perdus après lui, mais de ses compagnons, dans un gouvernement libre. (Original note)

28. *Lettres de Brutus*, dans le recueil de celles de Cicéron. (Original note)

29. J'emploie ici ce mot dans le sens des Grecs et des Romains, qui donnaient ce nom à tous ceux qui avaient renversé la démocratie.—Car d'ailleurs, depuis la loi du peuple, Auguste était devenu prince légitime: *Lege regia quæ de ejus imperio lata est populus ei et in eum omne imperium transtulit. (Institutes*, livre I), *Édition de* 1734. (Original note)

30. On ne donna plus aux particuliers que les ornements triomphaux, (Dion, *in Aug.*). (Original note)

31. Les Romains ayant changé de gouvernement, sans avoir été envahi, les mêmes coutumes restèrent après le changement du gouvernement, dont la forme même resta à peu près. (Original note)

32. Dion, *in Aug.*, livre LIV, dit qu'Agrippa négligea par modestie de rendre compte au sénat de son expédition contre les peuples du Bosphore, et refusa même le triomphe: et que depuis lui personne de ses pareils ne triompha: mais c'était une grâce qu'Auguste voulait faire à Agrippa, et qu'Antoine ne fit point à Ventidius la première fois qu'il vainquit les Parthes. (Original note)

33. Auguste avait établi les procurateurs, mais ils n'avaient point de juridiction: et quand on ne leur obéissait pas, il fallait qu'ils recourussent à l'autorité du gouverneur de la province ou du préteur. Mais, sous Claude, ils eurent la juridiction ordinaire, comme lieutenant de la province: ils jugèrent encore des affaires fiscales: ce qui mit les fortunes de tout le monde entre leurs mains. (Original note)

34. Voyez Tacite, *Annales*, livre XII. (Original note)

35. Cela n'était pas étonnant dans ce mélange avec des nations qui avaient été errantes, qui ne connaissaient point de patrie, et où souvent des corps entiers de troupes se joignaient à l'ennemi qui les avait vaincus contre leur nation même. Voyez dans Procope ce que c'était que les Goths sous Vitigès. (Original note)

About the Author/Translator

William B. Allen, professor of Political Philosophy at Michigan State University, also served previously on the National Council for the Humanities and as Chairman and Member of the United States Commission on Civil Rights.

He has published extensively, most notably, *George Washington: A Collection* and *Habits of Mind: Fostering Access and Excellence in Higher Education* (with Carol M. Allen), the forthcoming *Re-Thinking Uncle Tom: The Political Philosophy of H. B. Stowe* and *George Washington: America's First Progressive*. He previously published *The Essential Antifederalist* (with Gordon Lloyd) and *The Federalist Papers: A Commentary*.